A Geordie Scrapbook

Joe Ging

A Geordie Scrapbook

With an Introduction by
Brian Redhead

Constable · London

First published in Great Britain 1990
by Constable and Company Limited
3 The Lanchesters, 162–4 Fulham Palace Road,
London W6 9ER
Copyright © 1990 by Joe Ging
Introduction copyright © 1990 by Brian Redhead
ISBN 0 09 468730 7
Set in Linotron Sabon 12pt by
Rowland Phototypesetting Limited
Bury St Edmunds, Suffolk
Printed in Great Britain by
St Edmundsbury Press Limited
Bury St Edmunds, Suffolk

A CIP catalogue record for this book
is available from the British Library

The publishers would like to thank David Higham Associates Ltd for their kind permission to reproduce extracts from *A Tree with Rosy Apples* by Sid Chaplin, published by Frank Graham in 1972 and Macdonald Futura for their kind permission to reproduce an extract from *Up the Tyne in a Flummox* by Leonard Barras, published in 1987.

I'm grateful and will always be grateful for a Geordie upbringing, a Geordie twang and the Geordie sense of humour which has given me about sixteen million laughs against all the odds in this sad and sticky world.

And if ever I'm up against it – and I mean really fighting – I hope there's one voice around to shout:

'Gan on, kidder, get stuck in.'

Then, win or lose, I shall be ready to square my accounts.

Sweet Springs of Geordieland (1971) by Sid Chaplin

Joe Ging with his filofax

To the memory of Sid Chaplin who taught us all what it was all about.

Contents

Illustrations

Cartoons by Kevin Clifford

Introduction

I was having a meal one night recently with a man who, like me, was born in Newcastle, in what we would now call the inner city. We were in a country house hotel in the home counties. The service in the restaurant was slow, but we were in no hurry. We had not met before and we had much to talk about.

Having agreed at once that Geordies are the only people in the world who know that there are no hyphens in Newcastle upon Tyne, we turned to the days before the war.

He had spent his entire childhood in Scotswood, where, he said, he had an auntie in every street. He had only to knock at a door and it would be opened by a plump lady who would say in greeting: 'It's wor Ronnie.'

He would then allow himself to submit to a large embrace, confident that it would be followed by something to eat. He even had an Auntie Seppie, Septima, the seventh child.

The world he described was like a seventh heaven, and I recognized it – a world where you could hurtle out of doors in the morning and get up to mischief, confident that you were safe, loved, and watched over.

I told him about my grandfather, my father's father, who was always on my side. He believed that I could do no wrong, a view I shared.

My grandfather also believed that work should not interfere with pleasure. He was a provision merchant, as distinct from a grocer, and was always happy to step out of the shop to join a favoured customer in the pub.

He always went home for his dinner taking with him mounds of food from the market, which my grandmother, who was called Laura, would cook. There would be a mountain of food on his plate and he would eat steadily until, with a sigh, he would push the plate away, leaving perhaps one spoonful untouched.

'It's no good, Lorrie', he would say, 'I'm off my food.'

At one time he had managed a fresh fish shop in Bishop Auckland, where one of his regular customers, or so he told me, was Anthony Eden's mother. She was not prompt in paying her bills, he said, but he needed her patronage because he had a competitor.

On the one occasion I met Anthony Eden I told him that story, but he was not amused. I think he had Suez on his mind.

From the time I arrived on this earth my grandfather and grandmother lived in a succession of rented houses in Newcastle in various of the streets which ran down from Elswick Road to Scotswood Road.

One winter's night in the early thirties, when they were living in Clara Street, in the house where I was born, there was a tremendous storm with high winds and heavy snow.

The wall of Elswick Cemetery burst and coffins slid out on the snow down Clara Street. I was hanging out of the window watching and shouted: 'Hey, Grandpa, there's a coffin going past.'

'Is it anybody we know?' he replied.

Clara Street is probably the steepest street in Newcastle, and when war broke out they built a series of air

xii

raid shelters down the middle of it, like a giant staircase.

On another stormy night in 1940, my father, driving in the black-out and blinded by the snow, inadvertently parked on the roof of one of the shelters.

He opened the car door, stepped out, fell off the roof of the shelter on to the road and broke his leg. I thought that was funny too, but I was careful not to laugh.

Not that my father lacked a sense of humour. Years later I was given a beautiful antique oak stick barometer for Christmas. It was a good three feet long, and I took it to show him.

'It's very nice', he said, 'but how will you get it in your mouth?'

My mother too had a great wit. At infants' school I was always in trouble for talking in class. One afternoon, when I was late for some child's birthday party because I had been kept in after school to write out one hundred times *I must not talk in class*, another mother made some acid comment about my incessant chatter.

'Our Brian was talking when he came out of the womb,' said my mother.

The other woman fell for it.

'And what was he saying?' she asked.

'He was saying', my mother replied, 'that you would not believe what goes on in there.'

My grandmother, my mother's mother-in-law, chortled over that. She had been brought up in the music hall, not on-stage but backstage. She was Marie Lloyd's dresser for a while, and after she was married she took in theatrical boarders. Her favourites were Florrie Ford and Nellie Wallace. And she kept a bottle of port in the oven ready for them.

She once observed of one of my cousins, who at the age of three was given to standing on his head for long periods, that he had a different point of view from the rest of us.

My other grandmother, who was a widow, lived in Heaton, where the back lanes of the avenues were a network of backyard walls. It was a great holiday exercise to learn to run along the tops of those walls without falling off.

Years later in New York I was watching some Apache Indians, who seem to have no sense of vertigo and who specialize in high-rise work, running at speed along narrow strips of steel scaffolding hundreds of feet above the ground.

'Do you know where they are from?' asked the American I was with.

'Yes,' I said, 'Seventh Avenue, Heaton.'

It was wasted on him, but not on my supper companion.

'Wherever you gan,' he said, quoting, but fortunately not singing, 'you're sure to meet a Geordie.' And we turned from family reminiscence to recollections of professional Geordie humour: Sal Sturgeon, *Wot Cheor Geordie*, and 'The Last Bus to Seaton Burn'.

'We have missed a lot, living away,' he said, so I told him about Joe Ging's project, this book, and Joe's encyclopaedic knowledge of the subject.

I also told him Richard Kelly's famous story of Willie Walker's audition for the BBC.

Willie played alto saxophone with Geraldo for many years, and, when he returned to Newcastle, he formed a sextet to play at Fenwick's Terrace Tea-Room. It was where we went as teenagers on Saturday mornings.

The sextet swiftly became popular, and Dick invited Willie to an audition. The sextet played its standard repertoire, 'Blue Skies', 'Blue Moon', and the like, but

xiv

then finished by playing the national anthem.

Dick stepped forward, pushing his glasses back.

'I don't think we want that, Willie,' he said.

'I know', said Willie, 'but it's our best number.'

One RGS boy, who would pop into Fenwick's on a Saturday morning on his way from the snooker hall to St James's Park, was a great Newcastle United fan. He never missed a home match.

Asked afterwards if it had been a good game, he would go into an intricate mime – a flick, a feint, a turn of the head – and then a single word uttered in adoration: Robledo.

Robledo was one of two brothers from Chile who played for United at that time, but which one he favoured I can never remember. George, perhaps?

St James's Park was, and is, the source of many great Geordie stories. My favourite was the day of a United versus Sunderland match – always a tense occasion – when every time United's centre forward, a big ginger-haired lad lacking in subtlety, got the ball, Sunderland played him offside.

A man near me cried out in exasperation. 'If they hold their hands up any more', he said, 'they'll get their palms sunbornt.'

And it was outside St James's Park that I once climbed aboard a trolley bus, just in time to hear one factory girl say to another: 'We must've gettin' the sooner bus.'

'If that had been in Ashington', said my companion at supper, 'she would have said: "We must've gettin' the sharper bus".'

By this time we had talked for two hours, occasionally remembering to eat, and the waitress now arrived with the cheese trolley.

There were two dozen cheeses to choose from and the

waitress studiously recited the name and the place of birth of every one of them.

My companion listened patiently. When she had finished her recitation he looked at her solemnly and said, with a rising Geordie inflection: 'Have you any Kraft slices?'

I looked at him in admiration.

'I shall tell Joe Ging about you,' I said.

Brian Redhead

Here be dragons

1 Here be Dragons: The Unwary's Guide to the Territory

This is a guide for the intrepid traveller to hug to his bosom in moments of stress when the terrain terrifies him, the bizarre berates him and the language becomes more and more incomprehensible. No place for the faint-hearted, or even the normal.

Recommended starting point – Newcastle, the canny town itself, pronounced New-cassell, roughly speaking, as we do up here.

To the north is the Scottish border and the delightful towns of the River Tweed including Berwick with its Elizabethan walls and beautiful coastal views. To the south lie the industrial Tees and Hartlepool. British West Hartlepool, according to music hall comics, is where they 'hung the monkey'. Tradition has it that a French ship was grounded during the Napoleonic Wars and a monkey dressed as a French sailor escaped ashore. As it spoke superior gibberish to the Hartlepuddlians, it was hanged as a French spy. There is a song about this event which is not the official Hartlepuddlian anthem. The bowdlerized version has them cutting off its tail!

Even today this is a very touchy subject. When aspiring Olympic contestants use Hartlepool for basic speed training, they arrive in bus loads and go into local hostelries. At an opportune moment they yell, 'Whe hung the monkey?' This is a rhetorical question and the only known reply is a bellow of rage. By this time the trainee should be on his way, with a follow-up yell of, 'Start the engine.' He should be approaching the get away vehicle, as well as the United Kingdom All-Comers record.

To the west there is the picturesque market town of Hexham, 'The heart of all England' – a typical Geordie claim for a town forty miles from the Scottish border, which reduces southern England to its correct status (cut-off point, Scotch Corner).

South-west, Bishop Auckland deserves a mention if only because it's the home of our very own controversial Bishop of Durham. He may not be Geordie bred, but wor David will take on any amount of Goliaths as to the Geordie born. We may not always understand him, but we are prepared to defend his right to stir it to the last vicar.

To the east we have the North Sea. It runs all along the coastline. If it wasn't there, you could walk all the way to Norway. But that would possibly interfere with part of the traditional diet – fish and chips. That was BC (before carry-out).

A schoolboy's definition of the North Sea is: 'It starts at the end of the coast road, and it is very cold.' And that is in summer. When we have one. A traditional day is to take a trip to the coast to watch the waves lash the rocks and the spray join the driving rain. 'It makes a change even if you don't enjoy it,' as one tripper said. This is known as 'the hardening of the Geordies'.

2 *Geordie:*
Origin of the Species

The Geordie nickname is carried with pride.

'A Geordie is a Scotsman with his brains bashed oot.'

'The English divvn't want wi', and the Scots winnit have wi'.'

If Geordieland wasn't called Geordieland, it would settle for Ethnia.

The inhabitants and their humour have very mixed origins. A soap-box orator claimed that there was no such thing as a pure Geordie. 'Nonsense,' shouted a heckler, 'A pure Geordie is a mongrel.' This could be a sensible paradox, because he is a strong breed, likes to wag his tail, and is not always predictable.

The Geordie legacy goes back farther than most, in fact

Geordie - A Spotter's Guide *

The Club.

The place to find Geordie, and the home of the North East's other famous beer – Fed Special ('now a favourite in the bar of the House of Commons.) Note the top pocket full of Biros – a sure way of spotting a "Committee Man."

The Opinion

Firmly held. Strongly and loudly expressed. "All Southerners are pansies Who've never done a proper day's work In their lives. A real job or a night out drinking real beer would kill them!"

The Pigeons

A good racer is very expensive but a good investment – Ask the Queen, she's got a pigeon loft. (Does she muck out herself?)

Newcastle Brown Ale (Broon)

"Brown Dog" "Flight into space" The standard by which all other beers are measured.

TRIPTAN FELL CLUB & INSTITUTE LEEK & FLOWER SHOW

SCOTTISH AND NEWCASTLE BREWERIES LTD

NEWCASTLE BROON.

The Leeks

The sacred vegetable – and for good reason – at some competitions a prize leek can win the grower T.V.s, videos, washers or big cash prizes. (£1500 in Ashington.)

Flat Cap and Muffler

Immortalised world-wide by Andy Capp and now the supposed uniform of anyone North of Watford. (Now very rarely seen worn by anyone under 60 years old.)

The Empties

For the bairns (children) to return for money for sweets.

The Whippet.

Smaller, anorexic cousin of the greyhound. shivers and wees a lot.

* Guide to a Stereotype, at least 20 years out of date.

to the Roman occupation. If it is true that we laugh in the face of adversity then Geordieland has had more to laugh at than most. Take the Roman Wall – think of the laughter *that* must have caused among the local conscripted forced labour. A great big wall all the way from Wallsend to the Solway Firth. I suppose if the name advisers had known that a wall was going to *begin* there they would have used another name, but it was a fair guess all the same and must have caused some amusement.

The Brigantes, who were the Geordies of the time, thought they were on to a good thing when the wealthy Romans arrived, talking about job creation and regional development. But the Romans did what every government since has done. They said that while they were keen to develop the area, they were not actually going to give it any money, and called on the party whips.

When the Romans were persuaded to leave by the democratic process of the day, called invasion, Geordieland entered a development period officially designated the 'Dark Ages'. No jokes survive from this period but some scholars assume that the Dark Ages must be associated with black comedy. (There is always dissension among academics, it keeps the discussions lively, and the scholarships pouring in.) However, it is the consensus of opinion that the inhabitants kept their sense of humour – names like Ethelfrid, Osfrid, Endbald and Edelberga which are still used in modern Geordie parlance. 'You're an Edelberga, go and have your Osfrid' is but one. I can think of others.

Apart from laughing at each other ('So why do they call you Endbald?'), Geordie had a pretty miserable time, give or take the odd pagan orgy or two. And then the Christian monks arrived on the island of Lindisfarne – Holy

The Roman Wall

Island to the present-day locals with their well-known sense of irony. These monks were the alternative comedians of their day, no funnier then than now. A favourite act of theirs was to perform 'There is only one God', instead of, of course, dozens. This gave the lads and lasses a good laugh. Orgies were wicked, the monks said, and One God did not approve. That really slew their audiences – at first, and then, Canute-like, the tide turned.

One who survived was Cuthbert, a dead pan comic if ever there was one. He travelled about on his donkey scattering the message to all and sundry who promptly called all donkeys 'cuddies' in deference to him. To this day. He had some good acts, like living in a hermit's hut, giving no audiences. That one would have qualified him for a government grant in the performing arts today, but in those days – nothing. His encore was to stand in a stream in his shift for hours. An endurance test for the watchers *and* the watched, like viewing Australian soaps. He was sanctified. Today he would be certified. He helps the Tourist Board at Durham Cathedral now.

When the Viking funrunners arrived, things really took off. They encouraged the inhabitants to see the funny side of their rape and pillage, and a ravishing time was had by all. Soon, and in view of the foregoing, they had established the Viking Men's Clubs. Morale was high, spirits raised and Broonaleda established as chief barmaid. 'Viking' was corrupted, and no slur intended, into 'working' by a natural process of many years of raised spirits and ironic comment on the state of the labour market.

The Scots were always popping over. They were practically natives, well connected, at least, what with intermarriage and rape. Fun and lowland games on the border between Scotland and Northumbria (*not* England, if you please) had always gone on. Known as the debateable

'*Oh no! Don't say we're on rape* again!'

The Border rievers

lands, the borders were still debating in the finest
academic fashion years after everybody else had decided
who owned what. The border rievers had a great sense of
humour but one which was not widely appreciated. The
clans from the Northumbrian side would hot-trod across
into Scotland and steal cattle which they sold when
they returned. This meant that the Scots were short of
livestock, so the Scottish rievers would foray south,
shouting, 'For aye, sooth,' thus coining a phrase and
rephrasing their coins at the same time, by selling the

cattle back to the Scots. Needless to say, the neighbours were not happy. Complaints were lodged in the proper quarters, after the complaints had lodged in improper quarters for years, quite happily. The raiders were rounded up and executed, which pleased everybody except the raiders. So with all the goings-on, and Vikings, and people on day trips on Geordie Stephenson's railway, it was fair game for the Irish in the 1840s. Strong settlements were established on the Tees, Wear and Tyne, the greatest being the Tyne. Newcastle quayside was wick with them and this resulted in pitched battles and songs about the pitched battles. Quite indecipherable, even to Geordies, thank God. They go on for hours.

Jarrow and Hebburn was another Irish centre and still is – 'a little bit of Hebburn', as Tony Corcoran calls it. It's from here that the Geordie Irish nip back to Ireland and win all-Irish championships at singing, dancing, music-ing and general mullarkey. They've brought all-Irish words into the language, enriching it with names Like 'Shenanigan', 'Hooligan' and 'Mullarkey'.

The Tyneside Irish Centre has recently taken up residence in Newcastle's Gallowgate. Very popular premises, originally prepared for the Newcastle United breakaway supporters club. It went bust. So did the original supporters club for that matter. There must be a message there. The present club does not look like going bust 'as long as the Liffey's still running'.

Soon after the opening of the centre, Tony Corcoran was approached by a contingent from Newcastle's Chinatown, which adjoins Gallowgate.

CHINESE SPOKESMAN: 'We wish to take over
premises, please.'

The netty in history (with apologies to the Lindisfarne Gospels).

'Howay man. What y'doin', makin' ya will?'

TONY CORCORAN: 'I'm sorry, we've just got
                    them ourselves.'
C.S. 'We would give you a good profit.'
T.C. 'Sorry, they're not for sale.'
C.S. 'We would like to open a Chinese restaurant.'
T.C. 'No, *we're* going to open an Irish Chinese
     restaurant. (Pause) And we're going to call it The
     Paddy Fields.'

The Irish invented the Irish jokes, to lull the English into
a false sense of superiority.

I cannot make up my mind whether it's the Irish or the
Geordie that give the Geordie Irish their wit, or both. The
other evening I walked into the Irish Centre with a plastic
bag dangling from each arm, both marked 'Co-op'. I was
accused of 'coming the old Michael with your matching
luggage'.

And so it goes on, this heritage of sheer delight. 'We've
got as far as this. Nowt will stop us now. Haway lads and
lasses, let's make the most on't, while we can. It's boond
ti rain the morrow.' And it does. And nobody cares. It
always rains tomorrow. In Geordieland.

3 *Parliamo Geordie: How to Taak Proper Like*

Each part of the north-east has distinct differences in pronunciation: the south is almost Yorkshire, the west tends towards Cumbrian and the north is the language of the Scots, with various shades in between. Babel at its best.

A Northumbrian Language Society actually exists. Members are quick to point out that it *is* a language, not a dialect. New members are welcomed with open a's and rolling r's. The Northumbrian pronunciation is my favourite, and 'around the rugged rock the ragged rascal ran,' must be heard to be believed. The uvula seems to lead a life of its own.

Many comedians use the idiosyncracies of the various dialects. When Balmbra's music hall re-opened in 1962 in

Newcastle's cloth market, part of my welcoming act was to teach local phrases, such as 'Whisht, lads, ha'ad yer gobs' (quiet, boys, hold your mouths), 'plodge ower the claggy clarts' (paddle over the sticky mud), 'Haway for a hikey on the shuggy shoes' (come along for a swing on the swing-boats), 'divvn't ye swing on wor netty door,' (kindly refrain from propelling yourself on the portico of our convenience), 'divvn't drop yer dottle or wor clippy mat' (no pipe cleanings on the carpet, if you please).

The culmination was the phrase which made one an instant Geordie, 'Wey, yer Bugger,' first used by no less a person than Ethelred the Ever-ready when he stood too near his torchbearer fetching a rosy glow to the cheeks. It's a phrase which covers a multiple of meanings, and is as harmless as 'God bless you' in Geordieland.

This tendency can be traced back at least to the area's favourite clown, Billy Purvis, who died in his seventieth year in 1853. The national average was thirty-five. Billy never did things by halves. He would welcome audiences by talking in his Geordie accent, cajoling them to come inside. Then, spotting people of a higher social order, he would break off, and talk in an adopted 'upper crust' voice: 'And if you div not wish to be seen entering my temple of Thespis by traversing the raised frontal edifice, you have my permission to gain admission through the rear entrance, and may I thank you for your indulgent attention'. (This is what Bobby Thompson, one of our greatest comedians, called his 'ready money' voice.) Then returning to his former customers Billy continued, 'The fond gonniels, they canna taak proper like ye and me, thoo knows. I have to taak to them in thor ways, man, the ignoramuses. As I was saying to them, Bella, if thoo doesnae fancy coming up ower the front, thoo can always gan round the back and enter through – Billy's backside.'

This phrase, one of Billy's favourites, was much quoted for its memorability.

Over 120 years after Billy's death, a double act called 'The Dixielanders' decided to open their own music hall, restaurant and public house. It was situated half-way between Newcastle and Sunderland. Bobby Hooper and Billy Martin were not daft. They acted as hosts themselves, and Billy Martin used the Billy Purvis technique to welcome the guests – *after* they had paid. I said they were not daft. A rough idea of Billy's technique (it changed nightly, according to audience make-up and reaction) was: 'On behalf of the management, may I welcome you to the Dixielanders. Let's have a good look at you. What a motley lot. No, let's be honest, I have never seen a more motley lot at the Dixielanders. There must be nowt on the telly, 'cos you don't look the type that can afford to come to a place like this,' and so on. And the audiences loved it, and bookings extended to the dim and distant future.

After castigating all and sundry: 'Any mothers-in-law in? Oh-Hoh, come to the front, pets, and we'll have a mass hanging,' or 'I like your hairstyle, pet, did you come in on a motor bike?'

After insulting all the locals as to their place of origin, habits, morals, background (or lack of it): 'This will take you by surprise, electric light and carpets,' he would start on the foreigners: 'Anyone here from Londing? Oh, then, may I wish you a lovely evening, and when you go back to Londing, will you tell all of the other lovely Londingers what a lovely evening you spent with the delightful Dixielanders. Thank you.'

Reverting to type, he continued, 'I've got to talk to them like that, because they don't talk proper like what we dee, poor souls.'

Although Billy had known of Billy Purvis, he had no

idea of his material, and this was pure Billy Martin. It may give a hint at the local humour and its idiosyncracies and lineage.

Using the local dialect has its pitfalls. A laboured example, popular in local school playgrounds, goes like this: 'What is the difference between a spaniel and Mother's Pride?'

Answer: 'Two different breeds.' Try explaining that south of Potter's Bar. Or possibly even Darlington.

An impossible one for southerners, much shortened:

SOUTHERNER: 'Do you know any card games?'
GEORDIE: 'Ice hockey.'
SOUTHERNER: 'That's not a card game.'
GEORDIE: 'It's the ca'adest game aa knaa.'

I shall not even try to explain it.

AMERICAN TOURIST: (*At filling station*) 'Fill her up, and can I have some air?'
GEORDIE ATTENDANT: 'Fill her up, and you want some mair? I'm sorry, we've got nee spare cans.'

The American is still trying to work that one out.

Some jokes only work with a Geordie accent. Please practise these. When reasonably proficient, send tape with your credit card number for critical and financial appraisal. This course is not for the poor in spirit or purse.

DOCTOR: 'Can you walk?'
PATIENT: 'Work? Aa canna even waalk!'

GENERAL CUSTER: 'Are they war drums?'
GEORDIE SCOUT: 'Nah, they've got their own.'

CAROL SINGERS: 'Hark the Herald Angels sing,
                Glory to the newborn King.'
GEORDIE: 'Aa nivor knew there was a king in
                Newburn. Mind, aa hord tell of a
                couple of queens in Throckley.'

A comment in a canteen: 'The tea's ca'ad, and the coffee's ca'ad tee.'

Seen on the back of a car: 'Divvn't dunsh is, wor Geordies.' (Dunsh – to knock into. That's all the help you are getting.)

A useful phrase: 'Any on yer any on yer?'

(I say, do any of you fellows have a cigarette?)

Geordies tend to pronounce 'ing' as 'in' as in huntin', shootin' and fishin'. Nor is that the only resemblance to the habits of our betters. To wit:

JILTED LASSY: 'But he promised to marry
                        me.'
SYMPATHETIC FRIEND: 'Did you get it in writin'?'
JILTED LASSY: 'Oh aye, I got it in Ryton,
                        Wylam, Hexham – right
                        away up the Tyne Valley.'

Possibly the best exponent of the local dialect is Bobby Pattinson. Although semi-retired, Bobby is still in demand for his inventive routines.

One of his scenes is based on a misunderstanding similar to the one above. A luckless motorist is phoning the RAC for help. His car has broken down. After many very cross references ('Oh aye, I'm a member. I've been a member for a month. Mind you, I haven't got my uniform yet'), he finally gets to the nub. In reply to the enquiry if he is over-heatin': 'Over Heaton? No, I'm not over Heaton. I'm over Byker Bridge.'

If plagiarism is the sincerest form of admiration, Bobby is surely the most admired of entertainers by his fellow professionals, judging by the numbers who have borrowed parts and, in one memorable instance, all of his classic routines.

Continuing in the tradition of exponents of the dialect, Bobby gives what amounts to a talk on the vagaries of the local terminology: 'Hoy the ball ower and I'll kep it,' is fairly simple, but try 'Arty yer gowk,' for 'May I have the core of your apple, please?' on an unsuspecting visitor, especially if he is not eating one.

There are people who try to entertain by using Geordie words like netty (outside toilet) and expect an audience to be amused. Unless you are a Bobby, a professional entertainer who can make most things funny, it is really insulting to an audience's intelligence. There are individuals who will laugh at every verbal prat-fall. Pity.

Bob Bolam has to be heard to be appreciated. And now that his stories are being used by George McLean (with slight amendments), a wide area of Northumberland is being enlightened. Soon all the Cheviots and the Wilds of Wannies will be covered. Not to mention the Northumberland Language Society.

Bob takes the every-night bedtime story and knackers it. No bairn hearing these would ever be the same again. In the vernacular they are hilarious, and I have watched 'foreigners' splitting their sides, then asking afterwards what he was talking about. Much is lost in the translation, but here goes with an example, the opening of *Sleeping Beauty*:

'Once upon a time there was a king and a queen and they wanted for nowt they'd got. Except they had nee bairns to pull the place down nor nowt. Anyway, one day, the queen went for a dook in the Derwent and she came on a talking frog sitting on a clemmie.' (See Geordie dictionary. I haven't a clue.)

'What Cheor,' says the frog. 'What fettle the day?'

'Why, just middling,' says the wife, 'I've been wishing I could have a bit family.'

'Say no more,' says the frog, 'Ye'll have a bairn by the back-end.' (Before the year's out, in case you are wondering.) And so on. Hard work isn't it? And that is a translation. It really is a separate language.

The story ends with a lad from Alwinton hacking his way in after the statutory one hundred years. Fortunately forewarned, the king had stopped the milk and papers.

He gives Sleeping Beauty a kiss, Lad, before he had time to read her the telegram from the queen, she shot past him making for out the back. 'I'm fair bursting,' she says. Well, you know the rest of the story.

Let's risk one of his poems, and see if you can understand the last line. Any translation blunts the point. The rest is sort-of Anglicized.

Tea Time
Three fellas oot o' Rothbury
Went to Carricks for tha tea
The waitress come across like
For t' tek the order see
'Tea aa'll hev' says the forst yen
'Wey, put coffee down for me.'

The thord yen thowt a bit, then says
'Aye, aa'll hev coffee tee'

You should hear that in a Rothbury accent.

Bob Hedley, scriptwriter extraordinaire, has written on commission for many of the comedy 'greats', several of whom paid him. One of these (who paid) was Stanley Baxter. Stanley invented 'Parliamo Glasgow', a translation of the untranslateable, the unique Glasgow patoir.

When he was booked to star at Newcastle's Theatre Royal in pantomime, he decided, in an onrush of missionary zeal, to do for the Geordies what he had done for his native city. He wanted an audience participation song which would be perfectly understandable to the natives, and commissioned Bob.

Bob's favourite language is Italian. He is a Geordie. This is the result:

Parliamo Geordie
Warra boora stotti fommi ganni?
Wirra birra bacci fommi da.
Curra hevva tab, orra happni claggi slab.
Mi murras possin clays shill nivva na.
Gorra ganna skyul aminna hurri,
orral gerra skelp aroon megob.
Iffya tark leik cloggi betti
tivva cuddi inna netti,
yikin parliamo geordie justa job.

Bob Hedley

A reasonable translation into up-market English would be:

'May I have some solid sustenance of the region for
     my grandmother?
With a modicum of tobacco for my pater.
I should also desire a cigarette, or a halfpenny portion
     of caramel.
My parent on the distaff side is utilizing the
     domiciliary ablutionary equipment, and therefore
     she will have no cognizance of the fact.
It behoves me to leave immediately and hasten myself
     to my academy of elementary learning,
To avoid personal chastisement: to wit, a direct blow
     on my masticatory orifice.
Should you enunciate in the manner of Elizabeth of
     inferior mental attainment to a donkey in a
     personal convenience of an antiquated nature,
You will find that you can converse in the local
     vernacular to an exceptional degree.'

4 Poverty:
We Laugh that
We may not Weep

There was a very popular local wireless programme which ran for many years until the mid-1950s. It was called *Wot Cheor Geordie*, produced by Richard Kelly. In those days the BBC issued an edict to producers telling them what they could not have in their programmes. Perhaps it still does.

Lord Reith stalked the corridors of power, turning it off if he disapproved. This seemed to be a habit, and hobby of his.

Anyway, Dick told me a rough idea of what was banned.

Sex was out for a start. It had not been invented yet and the place was full of storks and gooseberry bushes.

There did not seem a fat lot left. Except – what was

banned elsewhere could be allowed on BBC North-East. No, not sex. I've told you it had not yet reared its desirable head.

Poverty and death – they were allowed in the north-east. I asked Dick why, and he explained that they were such a big part of the area's heritage. As our potted history so succinctly put it, they have been around longer than me, even. My own favourite humour, Jewish, is also based on these themes. (Jewish humour only works for me with Jewish exponents.)

An outstanding example of the Beaumarchais dictum, 'We laugh that we may not weep', occurs in 'The fire on the Kee', a song by Ned Corvan.

In 1854 a major catastrophe happened in Newcastle and Gateshead. A chemical works explosion laid waste both Gateshead's lower reaches and Newcastle's quay-side, the most densely populated area of the British Isles. (I used to say the population was the densest in the British Isles until a quayside dweller objected.) Beds were a luxury and anyway they took up room where people could sleep. Thousands were homeless, hundreds injured and quite a few dead.

Seven years later, in 1861, at the famous Balmbra's music hall in Newcastle's cloth market, Ned performed his song. Many of his audience would have been associated with the tragedy and yet the song is hilarious. It begins with Ned in drag, Danny la Rue, vintage 1861, looking for his lost son, caught in the fire. Part of his description goes:

His nose is neat and canny, he's a model of a nanny
  [goat],
And the picture of wor Fanny, oh, the nasty drukken
  sow.

As for his characters:

> A good heart beats within him, for he knocks the
>   pollis doon,
> He has two nice black eyes tee, and a mouth for eating
>   pies tee,
> Folks say he's not over wise tee, and call the lad a
>   cloon.

Anybody who knocked the pollis down had to have a
good heart. Different times, different ways. So they tell
me.
   As for the fire:

> How many serio-comic scenes were enacted where
>   poor people did dwell . . .
> It was fearful to see the poor old wives in narrow
>   chares and lanes,
> Picking up their bits of things exposing life, I'm sure
>   they spared nee pains,
> (with appropriate bending over actions)

And if you see Jimmy, tell Ned won't you:

> He's no scholar, bless the lad, but smokes and chows,
> He's partial to military movements, especially
>   Sandgate rows.
> He's got his militia clothes on, you'll know him in a
>   crack,
> Besides some stripes for good behaviour, but they put
>   them on his back,
> His appearance commands respect – have you seen
>   him ganning by?

The skin's off his knuckles with fighting, and he
    sports a big black eye.

Even today, in this area, I think you would be stretching
the limit a bit to satirize a seven-year-old tragedy. At
the time Ned had not all that long to live himself. We
laugh . . .

Considering that humour about poverty is part of the
local culture, it is not surprising that it was exploited
during the 1930s. The means test and the iniquitous
authorization of official snoopers into the possessions of
the poor gave comedian Albert Burdon the idea for one of
his funnier sketches. A confrontation with one of these
snoopers brought great reactions from audiences, especially in the north-east. Here is a sample of Albert's
dialogue:

INQUISITOR: 'Where do you live?'
STOOGE: 'No fixed abode.'
INQUISITOR: 'And where do *you* live?'
ALBERT: 'I've got a room from him.'
INQUISITOR: 'How much money have you got in the
             bank?'
ALBERT: '£50,000.'
INQUISITOR: 'Don't you be funny with me.'
ALBERT: 'You started it.'

That story is still current. As is the one about changing
the timing of the dole recipient's weekly call:

DOLE OFFICER: '£1.15 for you next week.'
RECIPIENT: 'Thank God. I cannot manage on
               one-pound-five.'

Albert Burdon

That has the ring of truth, like all good humour.

Richard Kelly (creator of *Wot Cheor Geordie*), tells the story of a childhood sociology lesson. The 'lady' teacher was explaining the social strata: 'There is the aristocracy, those people with wealth and power who run the country. And there is the working class, those people who do the menial tasks. And in between there is the middle class, people like you and me.'

And there were Richard and his classmates nodding their heads in agreement, 'with the backsides hanging out of our britches'.

The means test features in an ethnic nativity chanson – a Geordie Christmas carol. It is entitled 'The Twelve Days of the Means Test' and goes like this:

> *On the first day of the means test the guardians took from me the door from wor backyard netty.*
> Stop the music. Hands up all those who can define a netty – define, not refine. According to my dictionary, Chambers, it is an earth closet. No flushing, pet, unless you are embarrassed. And the men with the midden carts came down our back lane. Up with the flap, in with the shovel, 'Hello Bella, Hello Geordie.' And they couldn't even see your face.
>
> *On the second day of the means test the guardians took from me one poss tub.*
> Stop the music. A poss tub was the 1930s equivalent of a supermatic Electrolux Hoover twin-tub washing machine. But it only had two moving parts, the poss stick and your ma. So very little could go wrong, unless your ma took a wobbler – she wouldn't dare on washing day. And every Monday morning I awoke to the thump-thump-thump of my ma's possing.
>
> Mrs Dalrymple, who lived next door – four feet tall,

four feet wide – was a bundle of energy – a double posser, so she went thump-thump-thump-thump-thump-thump. So was created thump-thump. Thump, thump, thump, and is the reason why the obscenity chanters at the local football grounds are always on the beat. And when she was nearly finished the wash, all my kid brothers and sisters would be standing around, as they always got in after the whites.

On the third day of the means test the guardians took from me one clippy mat.

I have it on the best authority that these selfsame clippy mats that we learnt to dribble on as bairns are now being sold in posh Londing shops like Horrids at £400 a time. Before the war you could buy four cars for that. £400! We were wiping our feet on a fortune and never knew.

Just last week our neighbours from Milton Keynes asked us in to see their latest acquisition – a clippy mat. Stuck on the wall. On the wall! I said, 'How are you going to wipe your feet on that?' They had no idea what I was talking about.

You never put the mat on the floor straightaway, mind you. Where *did* you put it? (Pause.) That's right, on the bed. Break it in first, and get a good winter's warmth from it. *But* always take it out of the frame, otherwise you'll think your lass has grown a wooden leg. It's warmer than one of those French divets. It's even warmer than an army overcoat, according to wor Bob's wife. Unless, she says, the army's still in it.

On the fourth day of the means test the guardians took from me one stotty cake.

Now the Russians have their caviare, the French have their truffles, the Hungarians have their – have their – wash your mouth out. Oh, aye, goulash. And

The Stotty

What is a Stotty Cake?

One thing it is not, is a cake. It is a round, flat loaf — the genuine article having a small belly button in the middle.

Stotty Hoyin'

The Distance Event.

(Thrown discus-style.) The use of artificial stimulants such as Fed. Special, Pease Puddin', or Saveloy Dips is strictly forbidden!

The Target Range.

(Using a backward, underarm flick.) Competition is keen, but only a select few have mastered the intricacies of the wholemeal stotty with its unusual flying characteristics.

we in the north-east have panhaggety and stotty cake
and if you've never tasted stotty cake you should think
black burning shame. They're shaped like an Olympic
discus. In fact, wor Bob's wife's are useful for just that
purpose if wor Bob cannot eat them, 'cos he can eat
owt. When she lends him her teeth, that is.

*On the fifth day of the means test the guardians took
from me one laying-out board.*

A laying-out board is used to lay people out. When
they're dead. Before they've gone too stiff. You've got
to be quick. I mind when me da died. It was funny how
it happened. Not at the time, you know. None of us
laughed then, not that I can remember. It was a green
card through the front door. Me da thought it was an
invitation to the St Patrick's night dance and when me
ma told him it was for a job, the shock killed him. I
went next door to Mrs Dalrymple who keeps the
laying-out board for the Co-op. Best firm for funerals,
ham and pease pudden' tea, *and* your divvy. 13216.
What's your store number?

'Mrs Dalrymple', I says, 'me da's died, me ma says
can we have the laying-out board 'cos we're with the
Co-op.'

'Just sit there, hen, till I've finished pasting these four
rolls of wallpaper for the scullery.'

*On the sixth day of the means test the guardians
took from me one pitman's cracket.*

Now, a pitman's cracket is a three-legged stool with
a hole in the middle for easy handling – stick your
fingers in and lift. And me da used to sit in front of
the fire on the cracket and have a bath in the tin bath
that lived on a hook in the yard. Most of the time.
'Cos we weren't always bathing. And me da always
got bathed barefoot all over, 'cos the best and most

32

hygienic way is to bath barefoot all over. Sitting on the cracket. And what fell through the hole the cat got and me ma says that the cat got the tastiest bite in our house.

On the seventh day of the means test the guardians took from me one fire bleezer.

A fire bleezer is a blazer. Not the sort you wear with a badge on the pocket that says 'Seaton Sluice Sons of Suction' or something equally meaningful or the sort you wear with your yachting cap when you go for the fish and chips. No, I mean a fire bleezer, shaped like a Roman soldier's shield. A *fire bleezer* is stuck in front of the fire till it bleezes up. But it is a significant symbol in a Geordie household. It is a means of communication. For instance, when I was a bairn, sometimes my parents weren't speaking. It was better that way, more peaceful. So they used the means of communication – the bleezer. I mind the time my father chalked on the bleezer, 'Get me up at eight o'clock.' When eight o'clock came round, my mother chalked on the bleezer, 'Time to get up.'

On the eighth day of the means test the guardians took from me one set pot.

When I was a bairn, every Geordie household had a backyard. And in that backyard there was a wash-house, next to the shi-shed. And in there was the set pot for boiling the clothes in. And all the wives from the neighbourhood used to congregate in the wash-house and gossip. Hence the expression, 'the talk of the wash-house'. You could always tell the front row – they had legs like corned beef.

On the ninth day of the means test the guardians took from me one skinny whippet.

The north-east has three symbols. The first of these is

the whippet – the north-east's equivalent to the Royal corgis.

On the tenth day of the means test the guardians took from me one pigeon cree.

The second symbol is the pigeon which lives in a cree or loft and is looked after by a pigeon-fancier. A pigeon-fancier can always be recognized by his standard uniform of white spattered cap and boots to match, just as a boozer can be recognized by his green boots and rusty zip. The pigeon itself can travel from London to Newcastle in three hours – in the guard's van of the Flying Scot – and it can fly amazing distances in a short space of time, always finding its way home like an inebriated football supporter only straighter, much straighter. It has a ring on its leg, more precious to his breeder than the band of gold which he slipped on his beloved's finger all those years ago.

But time passes, especially when you are racing pigeons, and that ring is needed to stop the clock in the cree. The winner is decided by that. And it can take as long to entice the bird into the cree as it took for the pigeon to fly home. So the fancier does the traditional corn dance. This consists of eyes cast skyward, a tin with corn in it, which he rattles noisily in rhythm as he circles, and moves from foot to foot uttering endearing sounds such as, 'Haway, man, haway, come down ye little bugger, come down.' This is about as successful on average as an aboriginal rain dance. But colder, much colder.

On the eleventh day of the means test the guardians took from me one geet big leek.

The third symbol – a geet big leek. BBC Bristol, 'round the corner from the land of the leek, Wales, always makes its leek programmes in Geordieland.

And for why, but? Because Geordie leeks are the best, that's for why, but. Just look at them, with their fat bases and thick white stalks. Very symbolic.

On the twelfth day of the means test the guardians took from me one bottle of broon.

Broon is the wine of the region, a handy hangover to fit any pocket. Known to the canniscenti as 'Journey into Space', 'Maniac's Brew', 'Deliriums' Delight', 'Lost Week End and a Bit', 'Nectar of the Knackered' and so on, it goes back a canny while.

There was a Geordie, Christmas Eve, on his way home from the club, as steady as a dozen bottles, no longer bottled, would let him. And he had a duck under his arm, and the duck went 'quack', and Geordie replied, 'I can't go any quacker.' So he thought he would while away the walk with a carol. 'Good King Wonderlust looked out,' and the duck went 'quack', 'on the feast of Stephenin,' and the duck went 'quack.' 'While the snow lay roond aboot,' (and the duck went 'quack'), 'deep in crisps in the evening.' The duck didn't go 'quack' because a pollis, a big fat pollis, had hoven into viewen.

'Hello, hello, hello,' said the pollis, and Geordie looked around to see the other two drunks he was being nice to. All he saw was the duck, which had gone very quiet. 'What have you got there?' asked the pollis. When the duck didn't reply, Geordie said, 'Officer, I won it in a raffle.'

'In a raffle? Don't you know it's illegal?'

'Is it? They telt me it was a duck.'

And the duck went 'quack.'

On the twelfth day, etcetera back to the beginning. If you have the strength left.

5 Death:
Sting? What Sting?

There are so many jokes on the subject of death that it seems to dominate local humour. Husband and wife gags, for instance:

DYING WIFE: 'I want you, as my dying wish, to travel in the first coach with my mother.'

HUSBAND: 'I will, to please you, pet. But it'll spoil me day.'

DYING WIFE: 'When I go, I want you to marry again.'
HUSBAND: 'Oh, pet, don't say things like that.'
DYING WIFE: 'I want you to be happy.'
HUSBAND: 'How could I be happy without you, love?'

DYING WIFE: 'And I don't want my wardrobe wasted. I want you to give her all my lovely clothes.'

HUSBAND: 'I don't think they'll fit her.'

There are whole acts based on this theme:

So we got back from the crematorium, and put Fred's ashes in a glass bowl on the mantelpiece, next to Aunt Aggie's gallstones. The Co-op had done the catering, so it was a canny tea – the usual, ham and pease pudden' and things were going along well. Old Granda was spouting forth: 'There's only two things worth celebrating on Tyneside – weddings and funerals. Me, I prefer funerals, ower much crying at weddings, and I know why. Man, you can see all the troubles the young couple have got coming to them and it's no good telling them. And their ma's saying, 'Eeh, I wonder if it'll turn out all right?' With a funeral there's no doubt. It *has* turned out all right. At peace at last. Good old Fred. God bless you, sonner.' And he knocks the end of his funeral cigar off into the cremation ashes and others come up and do the same. Aunt Ellen comes across and looks in, 'Eeh, Fred, you're putting on weight already.' And then they found the note. Tucked behind the clock that would only go on its side on the mantelpiece. From Fred: 'I want my ashes scattered on Newcastle United's pitch.'

'I always knew he was a born loser,' says Granda.

So there was nothing for it but to go and get the hearse back and pile in. And off we set to the football ground. Then it started to snow. We struggled and struggled and finally got stuck in the snow. We had to use his ashes to get up the bank. Granda said, 'Let's go back, there's still a drop in the bottle! Poor Fred.'

Many are the stories about the mourners who come to pay their respects:

VISITOR: 'Doesn't he look happy?'
WIFE: 'He died in his sleep, so he doesn't know he's dead yet.'

VISITOR: 'He's got a nice tan.'
WIFE: 'We'd just come back from holiday.'
VISITOR: 'I thought so, he looks so well.'
WIFE: 'Yes, I think it did him good.'

VISITOR: 'What did he die of?'
WIFE: 'Of a Thursday.'

VISITOR: 'What happened when he – er – you know?'
WIFE: 'He'd just gone down the back garden to cut a cabbage for the Sunday dinner. He bent down, keeled over and that was it.'
VISITOR: 'Oh, Meggie, how awful – so sudden, like. What did you do?'
WIFE: 'I just had to open a tin of peas.'

There's a burial story about the grave digger who was asked, 'Are you the regular?'

'No,' he replied, 'I'm just filling in.'

And the apocryphal story of Robb Wilton and Charles ('Two Lovely Black Eyes') Coburn, who were attending the funeral of a fellow music hall artiste: 'How old are you now, Charlie?' asked Robb.

'Ninety-four,' said Charles, proudly.

'Hardly worth your while going home,' said Robb solicitously.

The funeral parlours have a life of their own, considering:

SATISFIED CUSTOMER: 'Thank you ever so much. I can't thank you enough. I wanted to bury him in a blue suit. He never owned one, you see, and I thought he would look nice in one and he does. What did you do with his brown one?'

KIND UNDERTAKER: 'I had another in with a blue suit. It was no bother.'

SATISFIED CUSTOMER: 'It must have been. All that changing of clothes. What a lot of work for you.'

KIND UNDERTAKER: 'Why no, pet. I just changed the heeds.'

Perhaps we should draw a veil over the subject.

And there's Geordie dying and his friends from the pigeon club calling to see him. There were two birds perched at the bottom of the bed on the board, looking at him. 'Thanks for coming, lads,' says Geordie, 'and for the two pigeons, best friends I ever had. And what a size – biggest I've ever seen.'

On their way out, the secretary of the club said, 'Poor bugger, I've no idea how the bords got there – I didn't like to tell him they were vultures.'

But their visit perked Geordie up, and he sniffed, and smelt something cooking. The aroma had wafted all the way from the kitchen to the staircase and up the stairs, past the landing and into the bedroom. Geordie realized it was boiled ham, 'Bella, I could do with a couple of slices of that ham you're cooking.'

Voice from the kitchen: 'Don't talk so daft – you know it's for the funeral tea.'

It's traditional; ham and pease pudden' makes the parting easier.

There is one classic Geordie death story, told here with detail not heretofore published. Many and varied are the versions of this story. I prefer the Geordie to the London one. You can make your own choice. There's plenty of them. No copyright, but everybody does.

Geordie died in London. Various reasons have been given – he was shocked at the prices, at the manners, at the pace, the difficulties in getting the broon. It all adds up. To save expense and upheaval, it was decided to cremate him in London – he'd never been a good traveller. His marrah, Tucker Johnson, went down to pick up the remains, the trip paid for out of the funeral club funds. So Tucker decides to see his old mate off in good style and takes him on a pub crawl, tucked under his arm in his cosy little urn. He even poured a whisky for him, over the urn. Just a single, not a double – no point in carrying sentiment to inordinate lengths. It gave off a canny aroma, so Tucker sprinkled the urn with beer and puffed his woodbine all over it. By this time, what with the occasion, the atmosphere and the smell of the urn, Tucker felt that Geordie was there with him, so he went on to doubles, 'One for ye, kidder, and one for me. No, it's my turn. This one's on me.' So no more drink went over the urn, apart from the odd unavoidable spillage because the London drinkers don't mind whose elbow they knock, or even who.

It was time for his train so Tucker picks up Geordie who by now was legless, 'I'll see you all right, sonner. Try not to jiggle me arm, it's gone a bit numb. Just hang in there.' And with various exhortations and a

'Good old Fred, God bless you sonner!'

little cajolery he got what was left of his old friend to King's Cross, where the Geordie train leaves London.

He found an empty carriage (it was a year or two back) and got Geordie and him two window seats, facing each other, 'Are you all right Geordie?' No answer. 'That's right, lad, have a bit kip. I'll explain to yor lass when I get you home.' And Tucker fell asleep himself. He woke up in Durham with a start. No need to worry. Geordie was still there. He hadn't even been along the corridor. Tucker thought to himself, 'He was a good friend to me, I'll just have a little peep to see how he's gannin' like.' So he picked up the urn, prised off the lid – eyes down for a full look. He had left the window of the carriage open and a quick draught blew in. It was no respecter of the dead, and when it left the way it came, the draught took Geordie with it.

Tucker took a minute to weigh up the situation. Then he stuck his head out of the window. No Geordie.

'To think,' said Tucker, 'the draught got him at last. He never drank bottled, you know.' But the air cleared his head a bit and he could see Durham Cathedral and the castle beside it. Most picturesque. (Nowt to do with the story, but grand local colour.)

What to do? As the cathedral disappeared into the distance, Tucker took stock. Not a drop left. There was only one thing for it, he would have to confront the widow Geordie with his sad news: 'He jumped out of the train at Durham, pet, to pay his respects to the Gala and St Cuthbert, and to congratulate the bishop on his latest outburst.'

At Newcastle Central Station, he hied it home and looked in the grate. Just as he thought, the ashes hadn't been cleared. He scooped two handfuls into the urn, and just stopped long enough to give their lass a clip for her slovenly ways. Then he set off to Geordie's home. His widow was ever so grateful.

'What can I do to show my appreciation?' she asked.

'That's all right, pet, your man's not long dead, just pour me a tot of whisky.'

So she did, then they sat down and went over Geordie's good point.

Mrs Geordie then said, 'Do you mind if I have a quick look at him? After all, he was me man,' which covers a lot of considerations.

'Not at all,' said Geordie with a glance at the closed window and a magnanimous gesture.

Then she looked in the open urn and said, 'Eeh, you know, that's all that's left of wor Geordie, a handful of ashes and two egg shells.'

And what is the present day attitude to deatth? (or even 'death'). It is treated with respect. It is, according to the evidence, fairly final.

However, Jimmy Butterfield had his own ideas. As you will see. He was, after all, a direct descendant of Cushie Butterfield (of Geordie classic song fame). After running the pub opposite Tyne Tees Television station for many years ('I was the fly on the wall. I knew more about Tyne Tees than their personnel department! [Pause]. But there again, who doesn't?'), Jimmy moved to the famous Crown Posada on the quayside.

Stories about his sense of humour are legion, so it was no surprise when his funeral hit the national headlines. It was *literally* a Godsend for the tabloids. This piece in the *Sun*, called 'Tribute to a Joker', was by Nick Ridley:

A rude wreath at Jimmy Butterfield's funeral summed up his laugh-a-minute approach to life. It spelled out his favourite swearword!*

Joking Jimmy's family paid £120 for the six-foot long floral tribute after he left instructions that his send-off was to be a happy occasion.

Mourners and onlookers almost died laughing as the wreath of red and white carnations was paraded in the hearse on the six-mile journey to the crematorium.

The fun continued at the service as publican Jimmy's coffin disappeared into the furnace to the strains of 'Happy Days Are Here Again'.

Then they played the John Miles hit 'Music Is My First Love' – requested by Jimmy because he had heard it murdered so often by club singers.

And the landlord's pal, radio star Frank Wappat, had mourners in stitches with a hilarious account of Jimmy's life.

Frank recalled how Jimmy once staggered into a posh restaurant wearing a flying jacket and goggles and asked: 'Where have I landed?'

Yesterday Jimmy's daughter Sue said of the rude wreath: 'Dad's favourite curse was spelled out in two-foot high letters.

'People were falling about laughing all along the hearse's route.

'One workman was so convulsed he almost fell into his trench.

'Dad would have loved to have seen the smiles on people's faces.'

Sue, 23, admitted: 'It was a bit awkward going to the florist to ask for Dad's wreath. The girl couldn't spell the word.'

* Bollocks.

Jimmy, landlord of the Crown Posada in Newcastle upon Tyne, died of liver failure aged forty-nine.

His widow Mary said after the funeral, 'He would have been laughing louder than anyone.'

Mourners at other funerals objected to the eight-letter wreath being left at the crematorium. So Jimmy's pals took it to his pub.

The article was on page three. Jimmy would have appreciated the juxtaposition.

6 Work:
The Curse of the
Drinking Classes

Work stories are as plentiful as promises to improve things in the north-east. There used to be a lot of it about. Hence the legends: 'So on the Monday, I gets up to stop off. I need time off to sign on' (Bobby Thompson).

'By lad, it's a funny thing, but every time I come in here I catch ye deein' nowt.'

'There's nowt funny about that – ye're wearin' rubber soles.'

An unofficial rumour that the north-east DHSS is to receive the Queen's Award for Industry has been finally officially denied.

There is still the mining tradition in the north-east although it is much depleted. Jack Elliott of Birtley was the local guru.

One of Jack's stories was about a pit accident. Among those trapped were a local preacher and a local agnostic. The climax of the story is the local preacher's decision to pray to Jesus Christ for help. The agnostic's reply was, 'Do you not think you should fetch the father in on this one? I reckon it is ower big a job for the young 'un.'

Bert Draycott is still a deputy in Horden pit, in darkest Bobby Thompson country. With the same accent, and the same gift, he performs in the local folk clubs. One of his many acts is about the right of women to work down the pit. He appointed himself the recruiting officer for female miners.

So I want you, now you've signed on, to report at Horden Colliery on Monday morning. You'll recognize it, on the right hand side on the way north from Blackhall. Where they tested the atom bomb and created £2.75 worth of damage. I'll be standing to meet you at the cage – you'll recognize it – it's just like the lift at Fenwick's. And when we get to the bottom of the shaft you'll be impressed by the lay out – a lovely wallpaper, fairy lights and chocolate coloured beams. Decor by a top West End designer who prefers to remain anonymous.

Now your lessons begin. There are two sets of metal lines called the 'way'. Standing on the way there is a little wooden box with a wheel at each corner called the 'tub'. This is moved by a 'putter'. He puts them in empty, and pulls them out full. Good, you're as good as the backshift already. Backshift? That's what you have to do with the tub. Use your back to shift it back on the way. But you might get some wet coal down your hoggers. Hoggers? Didn't I tell you? That's your regulation outfit – vest and hoggers. Vest? You know what that is! Aye. Even wor Bella's lass, Hannah, knows what that is. 'Cos I said to her on her wedding day, 'You'll be all right tonight, Hannah, with your see-through nightie on.'

'Eeh no', she said, 'he'll see me vest through it.'

Hoggers are like chopped-off jeans, so you look like a Great North runner. You can get these at various ladies' outfitters. The best buy is Purvis's of Blackhall, £1.50 and you can always take a club out – ten pence a week.

Now you'll notice, as you go in by, lots of coal at the sides. Do not touch it, you'll just confuse the deputies. They sometimes chalk on the coal at the sides, 'Do not take coal from here,' because it could be dangerous. We once dug six feet in, exactly where he had chalked. An easy filling, you see. Then we chalked, 'Do not take coal from here.' When the deputy came back, he looked, scratched his head and said, 'Wey, lad, it's just like Blackpool rock, lettered all the way through.'

And if you get a little dust on your lungs, don't worry, 'cos it's coal dust. And when you're sitting watching the telly, and see something that makes you cough, don't worry. My missus always says, 'Spit on the fire, Bert, it's £5 a bag now, dear.'

So now you're a putter, and you have to sing putting songs. It's part of your trade. Like this one, they're very short:

Put us a tub in, young 'un. In by or out by,
Or on the way or off the way.

And the traditional:

While he's in, he's out, he's off his own.
He's gettin' his bait, he's fillin' a one.

48

Off he goes away and then he's in, he's out.
And he's off again.

Apply to Durham University for the translation. They mightn't be able to hew, but they can translate like owt.

They're only short songs, 'cos you're paid by the piece. The more you put, the more pay you get. No time to sing traditional folk songs with twenty-seven verses.

This wet coal down the back of the hoggers. The putter's curse it's called. It scrubs your backside and can cause carbuncles, repeat – carbuncles. Only one cure. And you find out who your friends are. It's referred to in the following song. The only resemblance to 'Moonlight Bay' is the tune and the sentiment. I sing a line, you sing a line and so on. Watch my lips.

I was walking in by (repeat)
On the low coal way, (repeat)
When I heard a putter crying
I'm off the way. (repeat)

Would you give us a lift? (repeat)
'Cos me arse is sore. (repeat)
And when I get these two tubs put,
Aa's ganna put nee more. (repeat with feeling)

Now, there is a new invention to avoid the putter's curse. A wide piece of leather – two holes in – slot through belt. Technical term – arse flapper. Repeat. Where are *you* from missus? Durham City? This will be all new to you, pet, all this dignity of labour bit.

Now, once you've proved yourself as a putter (it doesn't take long), you can become a hewer. After about twenty years. A hewer hews the coal. He digs it

The Lambton worm – Wearside's answer to the Loch Ness Monster.

out, timbers the shaft and lays the rails. One action at a time. *He's* on piecework as well – one hewer on each shift – so that makes three. First or foreshift, back or backshift, neets or nightshift.

Now that you're fully fledged miners, you can all join the union. It's worth joining 'cos every now and then Uncle Arthur organizes things for you to go on a year's sabbatical – whether you want to or not.

Then there's the fishing industry. The North Shields fish quay is used to strange catches, from dolphins to octopi. None stranger than wor Tom Hadaway. He might dispute this. Tom writes tragedy and comedy with equal effect. Here is one of his lighter pieces. He says it is true. He would, wouldn't he?

Uncle George Willy

Me uncle George Willy, a coble* fisherman without benefit from his schooldays, would say disparaging things about the nature of education: 'Show me the book that tells ye how ti skin a skate.'

Me aunty Mabel would say disparaging things about uncle George Willy: 'Take nee notice of him son, it's all those years on an open deck. The wind has scattered his brains.'

So I had this mental picture of me uncle George Willy, sideways to an east wind, and little particles of brain streaming out his leeward lug. I would sit on the tiller flat with one hand cupping an ear.

'What's the matter son, ye got the earache?' I was just being mindful of my aunty Mabel's invocation not to end up like uncle George Willy.

'Divvent end up like yor uncle George Willy son. You stick in at yor schoolin'. That's yor place on the bus, yor chance to mix wi' better people.' I thought there was nothing wrong with me uncle George Willy.

'There's nowt wrong wi' donkeys son, but the' divven let them on buses.'

'A'll tell ye this for nowt son' (me uncle George was always tellin' us things for nowt), 'Ye'll nivvor hook a haddock with a pen nib.'

To an eleven-plus failure it was the ring of logic. I never doubted me uncle George Willy being the most thoughtful person in the whole world. He had this theory of fish, that they lived in towns, and villages. 'Jus' like folks ashore son, the' come tigether where the'll prosper.'

'Ye mean like North Shields, an' Blyth?'

* A flat-bottomed fishing-boat from the north-east of England.

'Exactly! an' in between there's nowt but wilderness.'

'But Whitley Bay is between North Shields an' Blyth uncle George.'

'What A'm tellin' ye?' The great mind never faltered, 'Haddocks one side, dabs the other, an' in the middle there's the lemon soles.'

Like all coblemen he was caught up in superstitions, but always with Reason at the helm. 'Green jerseys are bad luck son, get it off.'

'What's unlucky about wearin' green uncle George?'

'You fall off that tiller flat, an' A've ti bring this boat around ti seek ye. Ye'll find out.' His truth fell, and rose again on hills of ocean, emerald as the Cheviots. 'And another thing, when ye carry yor seaboots under yor arm, make sure the toes is pointin' doon.'

'Why?'

'Think of a drooned man bein' carried ashore, which way would his toes be pointin'? Thing is son, always gan oot the way ye mean ti come back.'

The direst injunction of all, never to whistle on deck, for it seemed, 'All the storms of life son, has a small beginnin' somewhere.'

Despite the careful following of these rules, and the circumspection of his ways, uncle George Willy fell into hard times, and had to peg his coble to Cullercoats beach, seeking work in the port of Shields as a deckhand on a Peterhead seiner. His return was morose, and grumpy. 'Bloody Scotsmen.'

'What's wrong wi Scotsmen uncle George?'

'It's all that superstition, it's got them daft.' Aunty Mabel seemed to be looking at something on the ceiling.

'A was the only Geordie aboard, an' first day oot,

there was nowt but bother pickin' up fasteners.' (A fastener was fisherman's jargon for an obstacle on the sea bed, like a wreck or boulder, that snagged the gear.) 'One after another 'til we were on the way to a new port record, ten hauls for half a basket o' fish. Then when the steerin' broke doon, an' the winch jammed the skipper went berserk. Gans dashin' aft, comes back wi' with this lang pole, an' a rag tied ti the end. Dips it in paraffin, an' puts a match to it.' Aunt Mabel was compelled to attention.

'So, wi' this flamin' rag he gans roond, an' roond the deck pokin' it into every hole, and corner.'

'What was the idea of that uncle George?'

'A'm tellin' ye . . . Scotsmen! A says ti this deckie, "Has the skipper gone roond the twist?"

"Och no he's burnin' oot the evil spirits!" A mean, can ye understand that? A grown man, in charge of a ship! How could he believe that was gonna do any good? Why son, everybody knows . . . the little buggas just run up the mast.' That's when I knew for sure my uncle George Willy was the most thoughtful, and logical person in the world.

Tom Hadaway

7 *Ray Stubbs:*
The Geordie's Geordie

When people ask, 'Where have all the characters gone?' I say 'Ray Stubbs'. A whole heap of them rolled into one. As Geordie as the Tyne Bridge, and some day to be as big an institution.

Ray is dedicated to irreverence and jazz, possibly in that order. And always available at the sound of a note, jazz or legal tender.

Ray also acts, on stage, films and TV. He plays Ray Stubbs like nobody else can. He plays nobody else. There's no need when you are like Ray Stubbs.

'Can you help me with a few anecdotes?' I asked him in the Crown Posada near the quayside. It sells Murphy's stout, to which we are both partial. I expected him to arrange a convivial evening over a bevvy or three and a note or two, him on guitar and mouth-organ and me on notebook. But no, he sent me a young thesis, entitled 'Work Stories'. Here are a few selections. They emphasize the survival qualities of an archetypal Geordie of Irish tinker stock. A survivor in a country of survivors.

Aged twenty-two, Ray knew everything, had seen everything and done everything. Mick, Ray's leader, read a piece in the paper. 'Fire-eater loses circus job – not dangerous enough.' The cockney, in the middle of his engineering apprenticeship, fell for it – he had been a circus fire-eater, 'for years'. An improvized torch was made from newspapers, soaked with petrol, and the cockney duly burnt his mouth. He was given the sack for carelessness.

There was then his period as a 'hashish' dealer in Lakeland. Hemp and nettle are the same family. So he chopped up nettle stalks and mixed in parsley seed. The local dealer said it was the best hashish he had had. Ray reckoned he was doing the public a favour by not getting them addicted to hash and because of the smell the public were convinced that they were stoned. The big lads found out and Ray and his colleagues had to leave town, selling their Parsley Empire to a weekend raver 'who looked like us but slept in a hotel'.

On to Ray's first trio with Ronnie and Eric. Eric was a hod carrier on a building site. A 'no cards job', so he could also draw the dole. He had to tip the foreman, to keep his job secure. He got greedy so one day Eric tipped him with a length of 2″ × 2″ timber. After that he had half a dozen Paddies roaming the streets of Gateshead for him. He had to leave town.

Music was all-important. An old mate, Paddy, re-emerged. He claimed to be a bass guitarist.

'Paddy turned up with just his electric bass guitar and

no amplifier,' Ray remembered. 'Me and Ronnie played our way through the Rolling Stones song book following the chords. We were amazed to see Paddy moving his fingers all over the guitar. We couldn't hear because there wasn't an amplifier. He didn't even have to follow the chords from the book. When it came to 'Not Fade Away' he flung the guitar, on a strap, over his back, picked up a tambourine and began beating time. Then he shook a maracca with his other hand. During a climactic solo in the song, he threw down the percussion and spun the guitar back around, his fingers playing up and down the neck. He got the job! The week after, he turned up with his dad in the car and unloaded his amplifier. He was dressed exactly like Bill Wyman on his latest TV appearance. We were so lucky to have Paddy! When he plugged in, he couldn't play a note. But he was good at miming.

'He was forever finishing off anyone's bait. We had a store-room that went back to items from the Crimea fleet. We dug out some "hard tack" biscuits from the last war and put them in a bag. After lunch, Paddy said, "Owt left?" We pushed the biscuits towards him and he ate the lot. He did say, however, that he could do with a cup of tea to dunk them "'cos they were a bit hard."'

Ray was not above a little moonlighting at one job. Everybody was at it: 'We were issued with reconditioned overalls of various colours. One morning the whole shop was summoned to gather outside the manager's office. All those who did not work overtime the night before were allowed to go. All those with orange, blue, brown or white overalls were also allowed to go. Only the blokes with green overalls remained. Then the manager said, 'Which one of you fuckers was running up the hill with a Mini-Cooper front over your head last night?'

The spray team were also the blokes to see for

Scandinavian-style fibreglass bucket chairs. We had made a set of moulds, and on our way around the ambulance bodies, we would make someone a set of four chairs. These were soon followed by an oval dining-table, round coffee-table, bedside table and a stool. I even saw two of the lads delivering a coffee-table on the back of a motorbike.

The boss, Mr Ward, was like putty in the hands of the shareholders, and the blokes on the shop floor got a hard time from him.

The factory used to belong to Decca Records and had two long tunnels down the sides of the shop, once used for curing the discs. We heard that Mr Ward was about to go on holiday and was leaving the factory in the hands of Chris Harkness, the chargehand. Chris was an OK bloke, so for a month before the boss's departure, we hid finished work in the tunnels and when he went on holiday, we booked the work through the bonus scheme. Production figures went up and Mr Ward was fired for his incompetence, but Chris didn't get the job, instead, they brought in someone just as bad.

With so many laminators out of work, a job was hard to find. Kangaroo Plastics were operating with a skeleton staff so Ronnie and I bought some 'fiddle' material via the back door and went into the coffee-table business. When I worked at Kangaroo, we used cardboard inserts from the mat to make the stem of the table. When it had a layer of GRP* on it, it became very strong. We had nothing like this so we used two empty beer cans – this was our treat every time we came near to finishing a table. We sold tables to everyone that we knew: relations, friends, pub managers, even parents till, at last, we had run out of

* A hardening material (used in Geordie baptisms).

customers. We tried a bloke we knew called Ron Bell. He had a second-hand shop in Gateshead, dealing in decent quality goods. Ronnie and I had bought several guitars and amps from him. Anyway, he agreed to buy a dozen from us and he sold the lot. The next batch didn't go as well. When we returned to stock him up, for the third time, he said he couldn't pay us any money but we could pick out any two guitars in exchange – so we ended up with a good electric guitar each! He had the coffee-tables for months, probably because every one that we sold had gone in that area. Eventually we had to change route to avoid his shop, and we could see him standing there surrounded by tables, like a pixie in a mushroom patch. He did sell them in the end and we still stayed friends.'

A government training scheme came next: 'I flew through all the basic work and when we got to design and application, I designed microphone stands and pieces for my one-man band. Most blokes were making pokers which I thought was pretty useless seeing as nearly the whole of South Tyneside was a smokeless zone. Making pokers was something I always remembered from being a kid. If you worked on a capstan you made pokers; if you worked on a lathe you made brass cannons; on a milling machine you made G-clamps; and if you were a sheet-metal worker, you would make a blazer (or bleezer). Other trades such as a joiner would make a fireside stool or cracket; a blacksmith would make a grate; and people in the building trade would always supply you with a well, or wall, or rockery, or crazy paving. It seemed that every household in the early 1950s had a particular sideline to offer.'

Then Ray got a new job, as a government trained schemer: 'My first day there I had a walk around during lunch. I got back into the machine shop and was going to

Ray Stubbs

start work when the foreman stopped me and told me that the blokes were having a meeting in the stores. I thought it must be about me but I found out it was a meeting to complain about the poor lighting in the toilets. All I saw was a lot of hands going up, and we were out on a half day lightning strike. Most of the workforce made for the Greenmarket bar which was open all day. At work the next day no one was allowed to start until the shoppies had checked out the toilet. The verdict was "bright enough!" and we all went back to work. There was a steady stream of workers with a newspaper tucked in the ruler pocket of their overall testing out the new toilet lighting.'

The adventures were thick and fast, like the acquaintance 'thrown out of the SAS for being too violent.'

Or like the time Ray was stopped by the police. The ex-SAS man failed the breathalyzer and they couldn't trace him on the police computer – his background covered everything. He didn't exist! So they let him go, knowing he was well over the limit.

There is a whole book to be written on Ray's notes alone.

8 Bobby Thompson: The Little Waster

Each pocket of the British Isles has its own humorists, who comment on the foibles, idiosyncracies and, dare I say it, peccadilloes of their fellows. Always in a kindly, understanding, loving way. For example, Glasgow has its Stanley Baxter, Liverpool has its Tom O'Connor and the north-east has its Bobby Thompson. You might well ask, Who? If you do not live within spitting distance of the three rivers, Tyne, Wear and Tees you may not be aware of his existence. (Mind you, we *are* canny spitters. *Spitting Image* has nothing on us, you should allow a lot of leeway.) Bobby did for the male image what Joan Collins does for the older woman. Think about it. If you want to know of his worth ask Roy Hudd. Bobby was but one of the legion of local laughtermakers.

Bobby Thompson

Bobby Thompson died in 1988, aged seventy-six according to the obituaries. His age is reckoned a little more by the canniscenti (the part of the Geordie mafia that can read without moving its lips). His time has died with him – the 1920s to 1950s Geordie scene. 'The dole is thy shepherd, thou shalt not work.'

The announcement of Bobby's death on national radio came as a surprise. He was only recognized as a great comedian in his native area, and, bar outstanding exceptions, who else could recognize his talent whilst struggling with his accent.

Reg Smythe of West Hartlepool, creator of Andy Capp, could have modelled Andy on Bobby, except that he had plenty of examples at hand in that neglected, sad town. Paul Theroux gave West Hartlepool a nil rating, but no solution. But Bobby came up with something: 'Stay on the giro. At least it's regular.'

Bobby had vivid memories of the 1920s and 1930s. 'War? Aye, wey, it's got us oot o' the depression.' To many the lesser of two evils. What a choice, not that anybody had a choice. 'I sees Hitler in the fish shop. He says "Bobby, if I don't hear from thon Neville by Sattidi, there'll be war on."'

Bobby was at his best in the 1950s under the stern benevolence of Richard Kelly. Bobby respected Dick. He knew that his rise from obscurity to a good living was largely due to Dick's support.

It was difficult with Bobby to know when he was joking. At times he probably didn't know himself, he was just a funny man. At one rehearsal he had to read about a 'coffee permutator'. We all fell about. 'I see nothing funny Mr Kelly, we've got a coffee permutator at home.' A bigger laugh, and a straight face, almost pained, from Bobby. Was he serious? We'll never know.

His wife gave him the name, 'The Little Waster'. For real. With good reason, I have no doubt. I first met him when I was doing the warm-up for a recording of *Wot Cheor Geordie*, my trial by fire, or possibly error. After I came off, Bobby said:

'Not bad son, where does thoo work?'

'Newcastle.'

'Newcastle? There's not enough work in Newcastle.'

'Oh. I just do this for a hobby.'

'For a what?'

'For fun.'

'Wey lad, neebody does this for fun.'

I should have listened to that advice.

At the time Bobby's act consisted of an imaginary family, all voices by Bobby.

One of the characters, effeminate brother-in-law Herbert, came out of Bobby telling a joke in the pub. Herbert put a pound note in the Salvation Army lassie's tambourine: 'Which hymn would you like?'

'Him with the big drum.'

'We can't use the joke, but we can use the character,' said Dick Kelly.

So Herbert lined up alongside Phyllis the wife, Zachariah and his missus, the parents-in-law *et al.* Bobby hid twenty pound in his boots and fell asleep. He woke up in a cold sweat. His boots had gone. The missis woke up, 'What are you looking for?'

'Epsom salts,' said Bobby.

'You won't need them when you find out where your money's gone,' said his wife.

And when he was called up for the army, there was Hitler's secret weapon, Phyllis's mother, 'God is good, he might never come back.'

The size of his wife in comparison to him was crucial. When the lights came on again, Phyllis had Bobby on her knee in mistake for the bairn. Bobby was half-way through the bottle. (No doubt Freudian. Ph.D'ers will make of that what they can, together with the fact that his mother-in-law, unlike the rest of his cast, never had a name.) The joke was believable, if you knew Phyllis.

Bobby's act continued with a trip to the coast and his comment to one of the other trippers, 'Meggie, pet, one of your breasts is hanging oot.'

'Oh, I've left the bairn on the bus.'

And preparing to go on holiday, Phyllis yells in her 'ready money' voice, 'I'm havin' trouble with the suitcases.' The string had come off one of the carrier bags.

Bobby Thompson's 'family': (left to right) Zach, his miserable father-in-law; his mother-in-law; Phyllis; Bobby; Herbert, the effeminate brother-in-law; and tearaway son Tadger.

'Wey, aah'm no engineer.' This classic remark is similar to one used in Irish acts in 1880s American vaudeville: 'Oiling the wheelbarrow, is it? What do you know about machinery?' The Irish influence again.

The 'ready money' voice was always used for pricking pretensions. Anybody who did not live on 'debt', the instalment system, spoke with a 'ready money' voice, or 'Geordie posh'. 'Parse the shugger, would youse, ta.'

'If all the catalogue clothes were taken off in here you'd all be nudists. I'm up to here in debt – I wish I was taller. And the rent man will keep knockin'. And he knows you're not in. Let him knock. Paint lasts longer than skin.'

Ignoring the advice of his mentor, Dick Kelly, Bobby signed up with the newly opened commercial television station, Tyne Tees. They decided to put his fictional family on view, with Phyllis his wife playing Phyllis his wife and the rest played by non-locals. It didn't work. One cynical comedian went as far as to say that the other cast members, who were all members of the *One O'clock Show* gang, deliberately sabotaged it. 'Bobby's tops roond here. If they knacker him, they'll knacker all of us,' was the reply. As though professional performers would do such a thing! Mind you, there has been a paucity of local comedy from the station. Perhaps the nation would not understand it. The same cynic observed: 'Tyne Tees Television did for north-east humour what the Vikings did for Tynemouth Priory.' It was sacked, in case you are wondering.

When Balmbra's music hall re-opened, I was a regular chairman for two nights a week. Bobby rang me: 'Chislett, lad, will thoo do Monday and Tuesday? Dick Irwin usually does them, but I've got a week's booking with agents watching on those nights, and you know how Dick can destroy a comedian's act.' I knew exactly. He had been King Dick till Bobby came along. If he didn't like a comedian, he would do a twenty-minute introduction 'accidentally' utilizing much of the following act's material. It's called 'gamesmanship' by yuppies. Dick was amenable. I was no threat. At the close of the Tuesday evening, Bobby brought me a double whisky. It shook me; Bobby was usually only generous with debt. 'Thon Dick Irwin can do what he likes, I've got some bookings at last. I'm on my way back,' he said. And he was.

For once the Geordie comic's curse did not apply: 'May agents watch ye while ye die.'

Bobby wanted on his tombstone 'Pay Neebody'. He died owing the Inland Revenue £137,000.

In keeping with local tradition, Bobby's funeral provided its own macabre humour. A local agent who had experienced occasional bother with Bobby's cavalier attitude to bookings in the early 1960s was heard to remark, 'At any rate, the Little Waster's turned up this time.'

Bobby, as has been remarked, had not been known to spend two pennies if one would suffice. Or better still, none. He had the odd disciple in the comic fraternity. One of these said: 'Let's face it, if there'd been a cheaper funeral going, Bobby would have been there.'

Two old dears, obvious fans, were overheard: 'Mind, Bella, he was in a bad way with debt.'

'Was he? Eeh, well, he's just got away in time, then.' Spoken with sympathy, feeling and insight.

Also overheard were two locals, who knew Bobby's weakness for the turf: 'Can you just see Bobby checking in with St Peter? I'm sorry I'm a bit late, I was waiting for the racing results. What won the 4.30?'

'Aye, and St Peter saying, "Who gave you that tip? He was no friend, Bobby, I could have given you a better one than that!" And Bobby saying, "It's easy to pick winners afterwards."

Bobby Thompson made no concessions to those outside his 'midden'. With an eager audience on his doorstep he did not need to. Who, besides Geordie, could understand references to 'debt', 'the club', and his love/hate relationship with 'wor lass'? – 'When she gets into bed, I get a shuggy.' I mean to say. Although, when he brought out an LP it entered the national charts, thanks to phenomenal local sales. He was interviewed at the time, on local radio, roughly as follows:

INTERVIEWER: How far can you perform from Newcastle, Bobby?
BOBBY: About thirty miles.
INTERVIEWER: How much further now your record has come out?
BOBBY: About another half mile.

Bobby kept his eloquence for his act. Nothing new, this inability to perform elsewhere. There was the time when Dick Irwin, local comedian, was playing the part of a pigeon-fancier. James Mitchell, South Shields – born creator of *When the Boat Comes In*, encouraged him to phrase the lines to suit himself, and one came out, in his Northumbrian burr, 'She's a canny bit bord thon mind, marrah.' The director, a little puzzled, asked Jim what Dick had said.

'She's a canny bit bord thon mind, marrah,' replied Jim.

Local clown Billy Purvis (1784–1853) was not able to travel farther south than Scarborough on the Yorkshire coast. He was welcome in Scotland, as far north as Dundee, because they talk funny, as well.

Stan Heatlie is chairman of Northern Arts, the oldest and arguably the best of the regional arts organizations. Stan could also claim to be Bobby Thompson's greatest fan. We were discussing the sad loss of Bobby, and Stan reminded me of the time that he met Bobby at Tyne Tees Television studios: 'You know, Joe,' he told me, 'as chairman, I've met many dignitaries, and never been tongue-tied. I was even able to converse with the Queen in a satisfactory way, from my point of view. When I met

Bobby I was in complete awe. I cannot remember saying a word.'

John Betjeman, late Poet Laureate and defender of all things Victorian, was opening the transplanted Rowley railway station at the amazing Beamish Open Air Museum. Stan's conversation with him went as follows:

JB: 'Who is your best local comedian?'
SH: 'Bobby Thompson.'
JB: 'Never heard of him.'
SH: 'He doesn't read your poetry either.'

Stan is a good chairman of Northern Arts.

9 Geordie Songs: Ancient and Modern

The Geordie heritage of song and rhyme is quite formidable. Wales, with its 200 songs, is known (quite rightly) as the Land of Song. The north-east, on the other hand, has thousands of them – traditional, adapted, or newly written, all available for the unwary collector.

There are composers who will write these at the hint of a barmaid's apron, traditional, adapted and newly written. And you can't see the join.

Take the earliest one, 'The Collier's Rant'. A story of a pitman and his marrah (mate) meeting the devil on the way to work.

I ups with my pick, it bein' in the neet,
I knocks off his horns, likewise his club feet.

You would think the devil would have had enough of Geordie pitmen, but no, not content with this, they meet him in the pit.

> The de'il got me marra, but I got the tram [coal wagon]

It was a shame about his friend but the means of employment was more important.

The song continues, like all the finest comedy, to emphasize the tragic side to life – the old miner no longer fit for work.

The earlier songs seemed to be associated with the sea or mining. 'Dance to thi Daddy' (about fishing), which became known universally after the TV series, *When the Boat Comes In*, is an obvious example.

This is a 'dandling' song to a child about the basic necessities of life – 'baccy' and drink. Like all such songs of the period, it is male chauvinistically piggish. Happy days.

A Geordie poem 'The Collier's Wedding', written in the early 1700s, is a bawdy account of a 'cultural event' by the town clerk of Newcastle, Edward Chicken. Bowdlerized when it was printed in a Victorian collection, it still has a raunchiness about it, and has the addendum, 'Rough scenes follow, possibly true of the times described; but of them it may be truly said they are now happily out of date.' Personally, I would not take bets. And neither would wor Bob's wife.

With the advent of the Industrial Revolution, which came later in the north-east than elsewhere, the songs and the acts changed. The railways from 1825, with the introduction of passenger transport between Stockton and Darlington, brought vast change in a short time. It also brought the birth of music hall.

Billy Purvis was still on the go, but not adapting to the changing ways to his advantage. One of his protégés, Ned Corvan, wrote a song about changing Newcastle, 'The Toon Improvement Bill', a neat indictment of town planning for the benefit of the few. It would appear that they never change, this breed of town and country 'developers' – a quick knock down, a quick knock up, and off to the next spoil heap. It is called progress, and we must all bow the knee to it, as Ned ostensibly did with his dry comments.

He came out on stage dressed as a small boy, using the name Bobby Snivelnose, no doubt to the tune of 'Greensleeves'. All the songs of the local music hall were written to traditional tunes or national music hall melodies. One verse goes, after a translation into English:

The Toon Improvement's made great noise,
But I heard my father say,
There was summick more than little boys,
Kept our wise heads at play.
There's bonny work among themselves,
But I must hold my jaw.
But still there's folks about here that heed,
The cash book with its flaw.

Ned's patter was quite inventive for the time. Here follows a rough translation of an extract: 'I heard my father tell my mother all about the town concerns. They thought I was asleep, but I'm a cute lad – I'm always awake when the tripe's frying for father's supper. I heard him say there were lots of rates, such as poor rates, light rates, sewer rates and water rates; but I think at any rate, there's no first-rates among them. But I'm losing all my learning now. What a headpiece I had at one time! I had to use a shoehorn to put my Sunday hat on, my head got so swelled with knowledge. Those days are gone, so I'll learn to chew baccy, me with the shirt-tail sticking so far out of my britches I can use it as a handkerchief.'

Ned was closely followed by Geordie Ridley, writer of the Geordie national anthem 'The Blaydon Races', a much overworked parody of an American racecourse song. His vastly superior 'Cushy Butterfield', is a funny parody of the cockney 'Pretty Polly Perkins', and close to the original in a bizarre way like all good parody:

> She's a big lass and a bonny lass,
> And she likes her beer;
> And they call her Cushy Butterfield,
> And I wish she was here.

To use just one verse, part of Cushy's description,

> You'll oft see her down at Sandgate,
> when the fresh herring come in.
> She's like a bag full of saw dust,
> tied roond wiv a string.
> She wears big galoshes tee,
> and her stockings once was white;
> and her bedgoon is laylock,
> and her hat's nivver strite.

He also mentioned that, 'Her cousin is a muckman and they call him Tom Grey.' Tom Grey lacked the native sense of humour, because he went looking for Geordie in Newcastle's Grainger Market. Such an affront to his dignity! Fortunately he did not find him, because I doubt whether Geordie's explanation would have been sufficient to placate him. You see Tommy lad, 'council refuse operative' wouldn't fit in and anyway it hasn't the same aura.

The last of this famous trio of song writers was Joe Wilson, a prolific composer. His story *Joe Lives*, written by Alex Glasgow, has been revived for television with RSC actor and lad-about-town, Alun Armstrong. A worthy interpretation, with Alun's humour enhancing Joe's wit and wisdom. Joe's most popular song is 'Keep Your Feet Still, Geordie Hinny' which vies with 'Blaydon Races' for popularity.

His description of a confrontation between two neighbours in a tenement, 'The Row Upon the Stairs' contains the best in Geordie insults from one woman to another: one woman finishes the argument with, 'ye paanshop-lookin' queen'.

My favourite song of Joe's is 'Aa wish yer muther wad cum' where Geordie is left holding the baby whilst his wife goes out for a minute. Ostensibly a male chauvinist song where the woman's position is subservient, it is actually a song in praise of woman's superiority. Geordie certainly appreciates his wife before the end.

There were many more performers in the same tradition before the turn of the century. One who got away was Champagne Charlie, George Leybourne from Gateshead. Harry Nelson, early twentieth-century, who lasted a while, had a distinctive style which can still be heard on old records. He was a top of the bill comedian in the north-east, but I doubt if he would travel south, just like all the others. For example:

CHILD: 'Mister, how much are your
                gob-stoppers?'

SHOPKEEPER: 'A ha'penny each.'
CHILD: 'How long will you let me suck one for a farthing?'

His songs included 'Hey, canny man, hoy a ha'penny oot', a tradition when wedding parties left the church, and 'Hev ye seen wor Jimmy?' This was a re-write of a Ned Corvan song which looks like a straight 'borrow' from Thomas Hood's 'The Lost Child'. Harry Nelson's version goes like this:

> He never cares to gan to school, he always plays the wag,
> And smokes a farthing clay pipe with half an ounce of shag.
> He tears great holes in all his clothes, he makes my poor heart ache.
> There is nee doot, when he's aboot, wor Jimmy takes the cake.

Harry Nelson also recorded a song by C. A. Weams, 'The Neighbours doon bela', the chorus of which goes, to a rollicking tune:

> Oh, they'll borrow your onions, leeks and peas,
> Whenever the pots to boil.
> They'll ask for ha'penny candles,
> If they cannot get paraffin oil.
> Whatever they borrow they never return.
> Such folks I never saw.
> They'd skin a rat for its hide and fat.
> Would the neighbours doon bela.

I'll tell you the doings of some of the folks,
That live in wor neighbourhood.
They're a lot of lazy good-for-nowts,
And most of them far from good.
From Sunday morn till Saturday neet,
They're cadging neet and day.
And whatever they borrow they never return,
So you might as well hoy it away.

After some punning about dogs coursing and people cursing (defensible in Geordie dialect only), the song continues:

They borrowed the dog for coursing,
and it came back just alive.
Then they borrowed a pair of blankets,
and they came back – just alive.

This reference is to a common household pest, only met nowadays in the homes of over-indulgent animal lovers: fleas.

During this period, J. C. Scatter was emerging, the man who popularized 'The Blaydon Races'. Nevertheless, he seemed a good comedian. On one record, as a female, he uses a 'Geordie posh' accent, when he slips, 'And the gloves, the gloves, when they start to go – they gan arltigither.' Always a popular target, the pretensions of the working class, 'ti taak propa, like'.

Jimmy Learmouth, the favourite comedian of J. B. Priestley, Arthur Askey, and many others, had a meteoric rise, and died tragically young. Descriptions of his acts vary as much as descriptions of the acts of Jimmy James – the comedy is in the eye of the beholder. Although a national comedian, there is no doubt that he used his

Jimmy Learmouth

native accent coupled with visual fun. 'Wotcheor, kiddars, how's your luck?' was his opening remark.

Wal Langtry, Frank E. Franks and Albert Burdon (C. B. Cochran described him as being 'the funniest man in the British Isles') were all in the north-east tradition. Then there was also a character at the turn of the century called Tommy Armstrong. He came from a town near Newcastle, called Stanley, and was a miner cum poet cum songwriter cum all ye. The Pitman Laureate's most sung song is 'Nanny the Mazer', about a trip for a pitman and his wife to town 'to get some claes for wor little Billy and Jane'. His wife gets drunk (there is always a first time), and they never get there.

Alun Armstrong claims relationship with Tommy. If they are not related, they ought to be. They are from the same area and have the same attitude to life, a peculiar sort of caring carelessness and both of them from strict non-conformist backgrounds. Alun refers to him as 'wor Uncle Tommy, writer in residence at Durham jail'. Tommy was no stranger to Durham jail for a variety of reasons, all of them legitimate. He was too honest to be there on false pretences.

One story is that Tommy, as bandy-legged as an over-enthusiastic horseshoe, saw a pair of bandy-legged pit stockings. Because of his upbringing, he believed in Divine Providence. He knew they had been provided especially for him. The judge, obviously of a different persuasion, did not agree.

One of Tommy's best songs is about Durham jail, surely not the easiest of ways to find inspirational material, unless, as Alun says, he really was writer in residence.

Tommy also considered it his duty to write about matters relating to the pits and pitmen, tragedy at the mines and protests at pitmen's treatment. As well as funny songs.

A few years ago a new headstone was placed at Tommy's grave in Tanfield cemetery, near Stanley. Such worthies as Tom Gilfellan, founder member of the High Level Ranters, were involved and he persuaded

Ewan McColl and Peggy Seeger to help in a charity concert. They were all present at the service at the graveside. The Rural Dean of Durham officiated. I forgave him keeping us waiting for half an hour at 8.30 in the morning because of what happened. Instead of singing 'Nanny the Mazer' or 'The Hedgehog Pie' or any of the other funny songs, Tom Gilfellan sang a lock-out song, of a significant nature. The Elliott family backed him. The Dean was quite impassive, I watched him. His thoughts were not visible facially – I remember wondering if he played poker. Tom was equally stony-faced later, and could not understand what I was on about. It was a remarkable morning, because Arthur Scargill stood for some time telling stories about the miners' strike. The Dean had gone by then. Arthur is not a Geordie, so I cannot quote his stories here, but his delivery, timing and material were as good as I have heard, and I love comedians.

Alun Armstrong, unlike many classical actors, is a splendid raconteur. When he was in Greece, he visited the Acropolis. There, in the middle, was a man who recognized him – he knew Alun's father. So they stood and sang 'Where-ever ye gan ye're sure to find a Geordie'. A much better Geordie national anthem than the present one. And prophetic. One verse goes, 'And ye can bet a silver croon, when rockets land upon the moon, ye'll hear a Geordie shootin' "Keep a ha'ad".' And what happened? First on the moon was another Armstrong, Neil it was, who has since visited the land of his ancestors, the Armstrong clan of the borders.

Alun has a delightful story among his extensive repertoire which is purely visual. At a party in Jesmond on the second floor, there's a shout up to the window, 'Can I bring up a crate of broon?' An eager affirmative is followed by a lengthy mime of a drunk being sick. Not for the faint-hearted.

Another of his stories concerns Geordie visiting London: 'Have you been up the Mall?'

'Who do you think I am, Superman?' comes Geordie's reply. Very 'in'. His *pièce-de-résistance*, which developed out of sheer boredom during the run of *Les Misérables*, is the conductor with no arms who still manages to control the orchestra with his remaining digit. Again, purely visual. He is, after all, an actor. His oral jokes are not all suitable, and we must press on.

Despite its formidable reputation, Sunderland has been a breeding ground for comedians and entertainers. Mark Sheridan ('I do like to be beside the seaside') was an outstanding example.

Wee Georgie Wood always claimed to be a Sunderland man. At fourteen, in 1910, he was the youngest person to top the Sunderland Empire bill, and was known as 'The Boy Phenomenon'. One music hall displayed 'The Boy Euphonium'. George accepted this; he admitted he was always full of wind, and could blow his top with little prompting. Stan Laurel, another north-eastern product, worked with him in his very early days as a golliwog, when this children's treasure was still harmless.

Georgie was 'big in American vaudeville', and had a command performance in front of Al Capone in Chicago. His description of the event was hilarious: 'A gorilla on each side with me in the middle, looking like an escapee from the chimps' tea-party'. When he arrived, he explained that he was a Geordie, which endeared him to Al. Apparently it was, at the time, a Chicago euphemism for homosexual. He went into his number especially dredged up for the occasion from his Sunderland childhood, a song about a little boy who went (raspberry) in the middle of the road. Capone was intrigued and made all his guests join in the chorus with Bronx cheers. It was fascinating to see civic dignitaries – chiefs of police and other local notables, who helped Big Al keep peace in Chicago – obeying his whim and losing all semblance of pride. Georgie liked the ironic.

Like the time he returned to Sunderland in 1945 and said to a favourite uncle, 'Do you know, uncle, two nights ago, I was performing in the White House in Washington DC in front of President Truman?'

'Two nights ago?'

'That's right,' said Georgie proudly.

'I never left the house,' said his favourite uncle – which was why he was his favourite uncle.

Georgie opened the now defunct National Museum of Music Hall for me in Sunderland Empire. On the way there the taxi driver said, 'Where are you going Mr Wood?'

'To open a museum,' Georgie said proudly.

'You're taking a bloody chance.'

Georgie was seventy-eight at the time.

After Georgie's death, Bob and Alf Pearson, also of Sunderland, took over as joint-presidents of the Northern Music Hall Association. 'I can just see the little fellow looking down and saying "It took two of you to fill my place,"' said Bob and Alf, in harmony as usual.

Dr Johnson had his Boswell, and so has the north-east, who does the same job but in song. No area should be without a chronicler, providing he is as fruitful and entertaining as our Eric.

During the 1950s, Eric was a staff writer with Chappells and produced pop songs such as 'Little Donkey' for Gracie Fields which changed BBC rules – no Christmas songs before December.

Eric will write a song for you at the drop of a hint. When I asked for a song 'à la Tom Lehrer', he immediately obliged with 'The Social Security Waltz', a ditty of great charm and insight. I suggested a song about President Carter's visit to Washington, County Durham and he was actually able to include Carter's memorable 'ha-way the lads' in the last verse which we then immediately performed on TV without an idiot board. I understand that is now illegal. He does not write serious songs for me, despite the fact that he said my voice was. Perhaps as great a triumph as any was when he was commissioned by the local television station to write a love song about Sunderland and he did, and it was. It is still sung, by people who are capable of singing it. Without laughing.

Joe Bennett, founder of the Northumbrian Traditional Group, explained to Eric: 'You know, son, you are the present-day bard of the Geordies, just like Joe Wilson was in Victoria's time. You'll be famous when you're dead.'

Eric's reply was, 'I can't wait.'

When performing, Eric appears to be accompanist, and the audience accepts him as such. Suddenly he comes to life, and takes the audience unawares with his quiet, unassuming style. He also takes them by storm, which always niggles me, as I have been sweating to amuse them, with much less effect.

Eric was responsible for persuading Catherine Cookson, through his music, to allow her writing to be translated to the stage. Quite a phenomenon, our Kate, and charitable with it.

This is a fine example of Eric's gentle Geordie humour:

I've got a little whippet
I've got a little whippet that never won a race,
But you never saw a whippet with a cannier little face.
She's just a bit short-sighted, and it shows up on the
   track,
But when she gets her contact lenses, man! you'll
   never hold her back.

I've got a little whippet. She's a wee bit slow.
And what it is about her – well, I just don't know.
She's not what you could call a canine beauty, I agree,
But I love my little whippet, and she loves me.

I've got a little whippet that never won a race.
Yes, I've got a little whippet that the pussy-cats all
   chase.
Her two front legs are rather short, her back legs
   shorter still –
So even on the level ground, she thinks she's running
   up a hill.

I've got a little whippet. She's a wee bit slow.
And what it is about her – well, I just don't know.
She never will be much good as a watch-dog, I agree,
But I love my little whippet, and she loves me.

I've got a little whippet that never won a race.
Something always holds her back, but what it is I
   cannot place.

I used to dream of having racing trophies on the shelf,
But it's no use my racing her – I find I always win
    myself.

I've got a little whippet. She's a wee bit slow.
And what it is about her – well, I just don't know.
She'll never win a prize at Crufts, I think I would
    agree,
But I love my little whippet, and she loves me.

Before the Coal Board decided that Geordie pitmen were
human beings their pit claes (clothes) were worn to and
from the pit and their state did *not* make them ideal wear
for 'gannin to carl on yer lass.'

Wi' me pit claes on
Last Thursday when the moon was up, I called on
    Sarah Dunn,
And the kitchen light was burnin' bright, I knew that
    she'd be home tonight,
But when she got a sight of me, she said, 'Ye'd best be
    gone.
Ye're not coming in this house wi' your pit claes on.'
But I got around the lass just like I've always done.
Sarah's got a soft spot for me. She said, 'I wouldn't
    do this just for anyone.'
So she lets me in wi' me pit claes on.

And when I got inside I saw the table it was laid.
There was such a spread I lost me head – man! no one
    makes such stotty cakes!
She says, 'It's no use lookin', cos me heart is made of
    stone –
You're not sittin' on that chair wi' your pit claes on!'
But I got around the lass just like I've always done.

Sarah's got a soft spot for me. She said 'I wouldn't do
   this just for anyone.'
So I gets me supper wi' me pit claes on.

'Now if ye divvent mind', she says, 'I've got to gan to
   bed.'
And she started trottin' up the stair – I started trottin'
   after her.
She says, 'Don't you dare follow me – I think you'd
   best be gone.
And you're muckin' up the stairs wi' your pit claes
   on.'
But I got around the lass just like I've always done.
Sarah's got a soft spot for me. She says, 'I wouldn't do
   this just for anyone.'
So I get upstairs wi' me pit claes on.

She called out through the bedroom door, 'Now just
   you keep your distance,
For I'm virtuous and pure and I'll offer maximum
   resistance.
If ye come in here me maiden virtue will be gone!
Ye're not gettin' in this bed with your pit claes on.
But I got around the lass just like I've always done.
Sarah's got a soft spot for me. She says, 'I wouldn't do
   this just for anyone.'
So I get in bed wi' me pit claes on.

Then in comes Sarah's father. I says, 'Fancy seeing
   you!
'Cos I just dropped in, like, for a bit.' I thowt that he
   would have a fit.
He glowered and he tore his hair. 'What has wor
   Sarah done?'

I says, 'Calm yorsel. I've got me pit claes on.'
Her father he went to fetch his old pit shovel, and,
 give him credit, he wasn't lang gone.
He held it ower me head, then he says to me, 'Ye'll
 bloody well wed her wi' your pit claes on.'
Here's my advice to everyone – never gan courting wi'
 your pit claes on.

And finally here is *the* canny fella song (Geordie dictionary: Canny fella – male chauvinist pig).

There's more to life than women and beer
When I was young me father wouldn't let me stay out
 late at night.
He said, 'Just trust your mother and your dad for we
 know what is right!'
And he gave her a clout 'cos she opened her gob, and
 he said, 'One day ye'll see,
If ye stick to the straight and narrow, ye'll be as happy
 as your mother's made me.'

CHORUS
'There's more to life than women and beer. There's
 more to life,' says he.
No doubt it's true, but up to noo it hasn't occurred to
 me.
'There's more to life than women and beer. It's
 obvious ye knaa.'
I'm searchin' night and day, but I haven't found out
 what it is so far.

Me Uncle Geordie said he had a bit advice to give to
 me,

With a beer in his hand, in the Rose and Crown, and
    Rosie on his knee.
He says, 'Alcohol is the Divil's own drink. Just take
    my word, it's true.
Just look what it's done to me lad! I wadn't want it to
    happen to you.' . . .

CHORUS

Wor Bella's uncle's cousin's elder lad thowt drinkin'
    was a curse.
And no one ever saw him with a lass. He said 'I'm
    none the worse!'
Man! Ye never saw such a miserable chap. He went
    round the bend, they say,
And these were the very last words he said just afore
    they took him away. . . .

CHORUS

I was in the pub – the minister was there – 't was only
    yesterday.
He says, 'Don't join those sinners at the bar, 'cos
    heaven's not that way'.
He says, 'Them that'll come to a place like this are
    deservin' all they get!
Yes, I pray for those wicked women there!' Mind, he
    hasn't had ne luck yet. . . .

CHORUS

Eric Boswell, ladies and gentlemen. Oh Eric, could you
write one about . . .

10 Working Men's Clubs: Are Ye Filleted?

A friend of mine was due to work as a variety artist (actors play) at Downhill Club, Sunderland. The club is well named, and one to strike terror in the heart of the bravest of performers. You even have to audition to be a heckler – euphemism for a club terrorist, paid up, of course. If they like you, they let you live.

He stopped his car at the barricades to the club area and asked the way of a kindly soul.

'Downhill Club, sonner? To perform? I wouldn't bother to go there, bonny lad, that's where the barmaids eat their young.'

One such occasion was a Christmas booking at Castletown, near Sunderland. So I called to see Eddie Angel

who lives nearby, and told him my venue. When anybody replies with: 'Now, I don't want to worry you,' you know they are going to.

Eddie told me about his own visit to Castletown. He had been breaking in a new act which needed the co-operation of a female from the audience.

He went down to the table where his assistant-to-be was sitting. She didn't seem very keen, but that often happens. It's part of the build-up. Finally, after a prolonged discussion, 'Eeh no.'

'Come on, darling.'

'Eeh no.' He grabbed her arm and pulled. Her leg was wrapped round the table. Over it went, drinks everywhere, dresses, suits soaking with booze. He was paid off. But first they took the cost of the drinks and cleaning out of his fee.

The dressing room was at the back of the stage, and he had to pick up his gear and crawl through hostile territory to the exit at the back of the hall. His suitcase kept banging into tables and he thought, 'it doesn't matter if you do spill some more – they cannot get blood out of a stone.' He had fourpence ha'penny in his pocket.

Eddie is a good actor, and I finished with tears in my eyes and a lead weight in my stomach. The club's musical duo (organ and drums) confirmed this tale and warned me to be careful 'because it's near Christmas'. I asked what had happened to goodwill to all men and all that.

'It's the extra drink, you know.' Extra? No comment.

Our Scottish tenor arrived and confirmed everything. He was not bothered. A good singer, he had also played football against Sean Connery in his younger days. 'Good training for the clubs,' he maintained.

He told me about last week's comedian: 'He was being heckled by the local hard lads – four of them, sitting in the front. He took them apart. When he left to go home he found they had done the same with his car.'

By now entertainment was my last thought – all I wanted to do was to survive till 'home time'. Surprisingly, the evening went extraordinarily well.

The Federation brewery or the 'Fed', as it is known, is one of the main suppliers of the clubs. Born out of adversity, the Fed deliberately ignored the professional entertainment, claiming it took too much money out of the clubs. 'Oh, aye?' said comedian Dick Irwin, 'You mean it cut into their profits.' I explained that they were only thinking of the future of the club movement. 'I've got a cat that keeps mice,' Dick said. The Fed even has its beer in the Houses of Parliament. 'It serves them right,' said Dick with a pint of Fed in his hand. 'Have you noticed how it's getting to them? They talk the same drivel as club committee men.' About as big an insult as Dick could provide. Fed is still a canny sup, mind, as Dick well knew.

The working men's club scene is worth a book on its own. As in all forms of entertainment, the club scene follows a cycle of success and failure and after the heady days of the early 1970s is definitely struggling.

Now, there are many empty clubs, presumably owned by over-indulgent breweries, 'closing like front doors on rent day'. So much so that the local branch of Equity, the actors' union, was obliged to change its meeting place several times in a short space of time through bankrupt host premises. One member believed it was more than accidental. 'Too many acts cursing too many clubs.' He moved that the next meeting place be a club which the members disliked. A wide choice was offered.

One of these was the now defunct Gateshead Labour Club, notorious for its audience-behaviour at Sunday lunch-time sessions. These are held mainly for heavy pre-prandial boozing and strippers. Eddie Angel tells the story of one such booking: 'I followed a young duo, boy and girl, who came off crying. Both of them. My first gag had a chant from the audience, "We've hord it, we've hord it," all the way through. Some of them even put their newspapers down to give the benefit of their judgement and join in. No self-sacrifice was spared, apart from slowing down on drink intake. I was reduced to singing to fill my time in, and avoid being paid off at half the money. I tried to explain to them that their shouting and chanting was their frustrated way of showing me their love, only their commendable shyness preventing them from showing it in the usual way. The worst of the lot was a younger man with a large plaster on his foot that went right to his knee.

He decided to pass in front of me on his crutches, making as much bother as he possibly could. It's called timing. Finally, I stopped singing, bent forward and said, "Were you last week's turn?" From then on I was a hero. A funny way to be one. It could just as easily have gone the other way.'

The concert chairman is the man in charge and you know what they say about power. A typical welcome went like this: 'You a what? A comedian? A comedian? (*sucks teeth*) Who booked ye? Me? I never did! Not as a comedian, any road. Did you say you were a comedian? They don't like comedians here, son. Can you sing? Oh dear.' And that is for starters. Tim Healy of *Auf Wiedersehen Pet* fame worked the clubs in his early days and met the aforesaid concert chairman, or one of his many *doppelgängers*. Being young and foolish he decided to go ahead with comedy anyway. The concert chairman told him to sing five songs, but Tim ignored his warning. After the interval the chairman came back to the dressing room. 'What are you doing second half, bonny lad?' he asked.

'Five songs,' Tim replied.

One comedian asked a concert chairman, 'If they don't like comedians, why did you book me?'

'It keeps the members happy.'

'I don't follow you.'

'It gives them something to moan about.'

The comedians in the clubs are the bravest men in the world. How ever do they build up an act capable of lasting two hours? And why? There must be easier ways of 'dying'.

When these mountains of tact get to the mike, that is their real moment of glory:

Ladies and gen'm. Before I bring on this evening's entertainment, I would just like to make a few announcements. It gives me great pleasure to announce the death of our secretary Jimmy Marshall. As you know Jimmy was a good servant to the club and his funeral is on Tuesday and there'll be the usual booze-up afterwards at the club for – what was that? Oh aye, the committee – forget I said that will you? Last week I announced the winning prize in the raffle was a diving suit. That should have read divan suite. Sorry about that. It looked like diving suit. The writing I mean. You'll see from the notice board that tonight's act cost seventy-five quid and I hope he's worth it. Oh by the way, I don't go in the women's lavatory meself, but I've been told that the tampax machine has been knackered yet again. Haway, now, lasses, if we've any more of this us lad's will show you how to respect private property. We'll move it to the gents.

The classic story is the concert chairman complaining about a noisy audience, threatening, 'If you don't shut up, I'll bring the comedian back.' And you know what a treat that would be. The following happened to a friend, who reported, 'It really was a bad night, completely out of hand. And when the bingo was interrupted the concert chairman took the mike, "Haway noo, lads and lasses, this is aaful, aaful. You know, you're even being noisy during the bingo. Aa divvn't knaa, can't you not wait till the acts come on?"' So they did.

At Humbledon Plains Farm Club, one Sunday lunchtime session, the performer complained that the inhabitants had read their newspapers all through the act. 'Never put them down once,' he complained.

'When they put them down, that's when you start to worry,' came the reply. That was the club where the star turn's name was put up in coloured chalk. Not to mention his fee (which of course, they did).

These masters of mayhem have a special way with the female performers and seem to think of them as personal property – one of the perks of the job. In the dressing room they can be difficult to remove. As one singer told me: 'There he was, God's gift to flatulence, entering and shutting the door behind him. "Do you mind, I want to change," I said.

"It's all right, pet, I'm married," he replied.

"Yes, but not to me. Get out!"'

Some of these gentlemen are not too quick on the uptake. And drag artists have been known to take advantage of this, for amusement only. One, who took particular care to look appealing, had his own technique. 'All right. Everybody out. You can stay.' And he was always first to go.

The concert chairman has been known to get his own back on unco-operative female performers: 'The next act has a pig's head grafted on, but it rejected her body. You didn't like her the last time she was here, but give the poor cow a chance. And here she is. Oh by the way, your bingo boards are on sale now.'

Sarah Williams told me of an incident when she was working in South Gosforth Club with her group 'Sandra and the Sabres'. As they carried their gear in they noticed a figure lying in front of the stage. It was a dead man. 'I suppose the evening is cancelled,' she said to the concert chairman.

'Oh, no, pet, he's not a member. The show must go on.' There she was with this body, by now covered with a blanket. Her first song was 'Oh, lonesome me' and her second, 'These boots were made for walking' with two stiff feet sticking up.

And what of the performers? Eddie Angel says: 'The foreigners, especially from London, have no idea what they're coming to. In the early 1970s they heard of easy pickings in the north-east. Plenty of bookings – yes. Easy pickings – no. I tried to help one tenor who had come on a week's booking around the area. It was a Sunday lunch-time. A stripperama was provided and the lads were waiting for red meat, fangs dripping. I thought I'd help the lad, he'd done me no harm. "Let's have a look at your music," I said. Opening number: "Girls were made to love and kiss." "You can't start with that," I explained.

"I always start with that. What's different about this place?" I opened my mouth to tell him, knew I'd be wasting my time, and announced him instead. He even went down among them, a Daniel he was.

When he came back to the dressing-room, not quite so full of himself, the concert chairman walked in. "How, ye, ye've got the peddler, half money, reet?" And out he went, a man who had done what a man had to do. The poor bloke from London hadn't understood a word. When I explained he said, "Oh!" packed his things and tiptoed out, straight back to the London train. "Girls were made to love and kiss?" They'd only come for the strippers.'

Ed Pickford's classic monologue sums it all up:

Death of a comedian in clubland
It was just after the bingo in clubland.
The comedian was dying a death.
The audience in droves were departing,
Leaving only the lame and the deaf.

On stage stood a lonely comedian,
A microphone stuck in his paw,
As down through the gaps in the audience,
He could see more and more of the floor.

Why had he become a comedian,
To suffer this miserable fate?
Was it his wife's greed for the money?
Or his mother who swore he was great?

Suddenly despair overtook him,
As he gazed at the vanishing throng.
Year after year it was like this.
Clearly something was wrong.

His suit was the best he could purchase.
His shirt and his tie were a treat.
How could it be they disliked him?
Perhaps it was his nose or his feet?

He put up with their crisps and their sarnies.
He smiled when they shouted 'Get them off.'
But now the final humiliation –
They weren't even stopping to scoff.

'Stop,' cried a voice from within him,
'Stay and listen a while.
One minute I crave of your patience,
Though maybe I've not made you smile.

I've tried like the troupers before me.
Our reward, just a little applause,
So there's no need to be extracting the Michael
With cries about me dropping my drawers.

This is my living, entertaining.
The audience is blood in my veins.
Without you there's no point in my staying.
On your laughter my future waxes and wanes.

For me it's never been easy.
This lad has been through the mill.
I've been beaten up in Bradford. I've been booed off in
    Bootle.
I was attacked by a whippet in Rhyl.

But I've had it. I'm finished. I'm done for.
You've proved that with a vengeance tonight.
The minute that meat pie connected,
Suddenly, as they say, there was light.

The wife and the kids, don't worry about them.
They'll get by with nothing to eat.
Why should you worry if they go to bed hungry,
Or have no little shoes for their feet.

Go off to the lounge, get a skin full.
Buy a few more to take out.
Go home, feed your faces, forget about me.
I'm not even worth bothering about.'

The room was all silent and waiting.
Then punctuated by a spasmodic cough,
The concert chairman leaned forward all tearful,
and said, 'Right, you're paid off.'

With only half fee in his pocket,
Stood the comedian in the car-park alone.
His career behind him in ruins,
As he mounted his bike to ride home.

Half crazed by depression and failure,
Ashamed that he's caused such a fuss,
He swept out of the car-park,
Straight under the twenty-three bus.

As he lay there in the glare of the headlights,
The rains beginning to fall,
He said 'Thank you for being such a wonderful
    audience.
Goodnight and God bless one and all.'

11 Geordie Jokes: A Very Common Heritage

When Balmbra's music hall re-opened on the centenary of its mention in the song 'The Blaydon Races' ('we took the bus from Balmbra's, and she was heavy-laden') in 1962, it became the Mecca for local performers. It was a privilege to work there – and that is all it was. As Dick Irwin, one of the original chairmen, said: 'It costs me money to work here. By the time I've downed my regulation chairman's pints, I'm out of pocket.'

But it paid off, because Dick got a new comedy routine every week. It took some time for the comedians to suss this. When they did, one took him to task: 'I hear you used my act at Coxlodge Club last week,' he challenged.

'It was your act? I might have known. I died the death.'

Dick always had a way with complaints, on or offstage.

Another time, two local comedians were having an argument in Balmbra's as to ownership of a joke. One maintained it was his by right of usage, the other by right of lineage. The second said that it had been given him by its originator, J. C. Scatter.

The gist of the disputed gem was that two Geordies were arguing whether it was the sun or the moon they could see. Eventually, they turned to a passing Irishman. 'Paddy, is that the sun or the moon?'

'How should I know?' he replied. 'I'm a stranger 'round here.'

I did not wish to be drawn into such a highly academic dispute, or I would have told them that my first recollection of the joke was in a book about Newcastle dating back to the 1850s. I preferred the original version, which took its time about things – practically a short story.

Like anywhere else in the British Isles, the stories are common property, and the jokes belong to whoever uses them that evening. It is not uncommon, should there be more than one comedian appearing at the same venue, for one to ask the other if he would mind keeping off such-and-such a gag.

I was once watching a comedian who switched in the middle of a story. His whole act seemed to change gear. I asked him in the dressing room if his memory had failed him.

'No', he said, laughing, 'nor my eyesight either. Big so-and-so walked in just then. It's his gag.'

'What makes you think it's his gag?'

'He's bigger than me.'

Much Geordie humour seems to be the joy of recognition, the happiness of the familiar. Do not be too original, but keep the mixture as before, like telling a children's bedtime story: 'Daddy, you missed out about Little Red Riding Hood saying, "Gran'ma, what a big nose you've got."'

I was able to exploit this love of the familiar at Balmbra's music hall by advising the audience that, should they hear a joke they had not heard before, they could complain to the management. It would do them no good, but they could complain. They never did.

An important ingredient, familiarity. It kept music hall performers going for forty years, using the same material around the country.

Jimmy James from Stockton who could give a cigarette a life of its own between his lips, was appearing at Newcastle Empire with his company – Eli Wood as the singing lighthouse keeper, or whatever that week's 'discovery' was, and the 'Are you putting it round that I'm barmy?' man. All of Jimmy's sketches were set in aspic, and the audience probably knew them by heart. On this occasion Jimmy put in a new gag. One of my friends stood up in the circle and yelled, 'Sir, you should be ashamed of yourself!' Jimmy James had the grace to come forward to the footlights, remove his trilby and say 'Sir, I am.'

Jimmy, a teetotaller, was a famous music hall drunk! His one weakness, however, was the horses, and he subscribed generously to the Bookies' Benevolent Fund.

According to Don Ross, a former King Rat of the Ancient Order of Water Rats, Jimmy was bankrupted three times by the Inland Revenue because his funds, and the Inland Revenue's share, had been diverted. At the third hearing, after the adjudication, he looked at the official receiver and said, 'Does this mean I now own you outright?'

Some of today's alternative comedians show great promise, once they realize that aggression does not necessarily make up for experience. It is fascinating to sit and tick off the old gags, not even in a new guise in some instances – 'Oh yes, Robb Wilton 1941, Sid Field 1944, Tommy Trinder 1943'. Teenagers find this very irritating because it is all brand new to them. A comedian who keeps going for twenty years can find he can use his original material as original material.

One of my favourite stories concerns some of my local comedian friends who realize the swappability of material better than anyone. Brian Lewis (of *Supergran* fame) was in hospital. Naturally, some of his visitors were comedians who are always partial to grapes.

Malcolm J. White was working away at the time, but he sent Brian a 'get well' card with the note, 'Do not worry about your act, Spike Rawlings will keep it going for you.'

The following are a selection of the community comedy loved by all, told by all, in their own particular style. Please join in the punch lines. You will know the punch lines – that is when the comedian gets that pleading look in his eye and a sob in his voice.

I don't even know what category to put this story in. I could suggest making it a floater,* which would be fairly safe today, the state of brewing being what it is.

---

* An item, possibly a hop, possibly not, to be seen in real ale (not real ale as in modern yuppy drinking – 'I say, this *is* real ale – as clear as mud and just as tasty – ha ha what?') when the brewery night shift had an even bigger hangover than usual and forgot to strain the brew through their lasses' tights. A declaration of a floater in the beer could ruin an evening for the entire bar. A false declaration could ruin the evening for the declaimant, depending on who hit him first.

A Big Daft Lad Loose in London and his Marrah
Two Geordie lads were in London to see Newcastle
United win the cup.

It was a long time ago. They did all the usual things,
like shouting Geordie words in the tube to show their
sophisticated attitude to life, and being sick in Piccadilly.
('It couldn't be the beer, kiddar, it wouldn't make a pig
sick. It must have been that crisp. I knew it was suspect
when I got it for nowt on the bar counter.')

The upshot was, they missed their special train home.
A passing lady, a real one, with her own home and
everything, took pity on them. Especially Big Jonty, she
felt especially sorry for him. So much so that, on entering
her premises where Jonty's friend, Tichy, immediately
flaked out on the settee, she suggested a conducted tour.
Big Jonty liked looking at new places and having new
experiences, so he fell in, so to speak. After all, there
aren't many London house tours in North Shields going
for nowt.

It only seemed to tour as far as her bedroom, but,
again, Big Jonty was very interested in bedrooms, he slept
in one himself. When he and the wife were speaking and
that, you know how it is. And he liked looking at new
places and having new experiences.

Five months later, to the day, Tichy confronted him. It
was in the club, during a darts match, so Jonty knew it
was serious and even stopped watching. His drinking
arm remained on automatic pilot.

The following conversation ensued:

TICHY: 'How, Jonty, do you remember being in
London with me?'
JONTY: 'Tichy lad, do I remember? I even remember
who won.'

TICHY: 'Did you score?'

JONTY: 'As I recall, *we* were on the terraces and wor Jackie scored. I'll take you through, step by step.'

TICHY: 'When we went home with that wife, can you remember what happened?'

JONTY: 'I have certain vague recollections of a lady with a heart of gold allowing us to share her home.'

TICHY: 'Did you – er?'

JONTY: 'Tichy, lad, it is never a gentleman's way to tell of his conquests.'

TICHY: 'Never mind that. Did you give her my name?'

JONTY: 'It is possible my mind was not as clear as it should have been.'

TICHY: 'And my address?'

JONTY: 'It may have slipped past my lips.'

TICHY: 'I thought so.'

JONTY: 'Have there been any developments?'

TICHY: 'I'll say. She's just died and left me £10,000.'

As you can imagine, the locals are in awe of their betters. And there are many stories to bear this out. Such as Geordie going for a job as a footman in one of the many stately piles (in the decorous sense) which grace the Northumbrian countryside and Newcastle quayside, to name but two.

Respect For One's Betters

After finding his way to the tradesman's entrance with difficulty, Geordie was escorted to the heed bummer (head butler). 'May I see your hands? You will be serving at table,' said the butler. Geordie obliged, apologizing for the stains. He'd just been feeding his leeks.

'May I see your legs. You'll be wearing knee britches.'

Geordie baulked at this, his bare legs were not a pleasant sight, and he suffered from wind on his chapped buttocks.

After sorting that out the butler said that there was only one further detail.

'I need to see your testimonials, you will be serving ladies of titular distinction.'

When Geordie arrived home, he explained, 'If only I'd been better educated, I'd have got that job.'

The next story has a long history. At least the Boer War. At least, although the more prevalent versions date from the Second World War.

Durham Gala Day: Canny Day for it

Two Geordie miners were volunteers for the Pioneer Corps. They had to be volunteers, mining was a reserved occupation. And what a war they had had. Digging trenches all over France, digging trenches at Dunkirk, evacuated, digging trenches all over southern England. As one remarked, 'If I'd know it was as easy as this, I'd have joined the army years ago.' The other one nodded. So off they went to North Africa, part of the Eighth Army, back and forth along the North African coastline, digging their way to victory.

'This is just like when we were bairns at Whitley Bay – sand castles and that,' one remarked. The other one nodded.

'Hell of a wide beach, mind.' The other one nodded.

Then the voluble one had a flash of realization. 'D'ye knaa what day it is?' The other one shook his head.

'It's Durham Miners' Gala Day.'

Then he looked at the sun and the blue sky, and

'I shall have to examine your testimonials.'

pronounced, 'Mind, they've got a canny day for it.' The other one nodded.

The aforesaid two pitmen went for their medical for an easier life, being shot at, bombarded and generally harassed. 'It's only now and then, not like a whole shift doon the pit,' one reasoned. They passed their medicals with spinning pit-wheels, the medical man remembering to duck for the second one when he asked him to cough. Two showers of coal dust in one day are two too many. At the selection board the two lads decided against commissions. 'A straight wage will do, thanks, till we get the hang on't'. 'And we don't want to be court martials either, for the same reason.'

After glancing at their legs, suitable for casting horseshoes, the board decided the obvious choice was the cavalry. This was a decision they baulked at.

'It's like this, you see. It's all very well gannin' forwards, like. In fact, I could quite fancy that. Heigh-ho Silver and that. But suppose they turn round, and charge us. I mean, when we're retreating, I don't want to be hampered by a bluddy horse.' He actually said 'Gallowa'. But horse is more universal.

12 Sport:
Alternative Religion

This is an area which produces footballers, runners and sportsmen generally, like turning on the tap with the old drip and squirt to remind us that all that glitters does not produce gold or even silver or bronze.

The locals will bet on anything, from the Grand National, pigeons or whippets to two little laddies disporting themselves in the school playground.

In the late 1940s a preacher from Coxlodge with a rich burr to his accent, and a loud suit à la Max Miller, was standing at the corner of the street, when a man came up and slipped some money and a note into his pocket. 'He thowt I was a bookie,' the preacher explained. 'God forgive us, I put it in the missionary box.'

You wouldn't think of leek growing as a sport. It is,

and a blood sport at that. Quite apart from using blood to feed them on, anyone caught interfering with a specialist's leeks will find out how much of a blood sport the growing of them is.

Swimming in the North Sea is recognized, not only as a sport, but also as a form of birth control. It is freezing. Whitley Bay Panama Swimming Club does this all the year round. Obviously, it is dying out. One of its members was giving a talk about its history to a local Women's Institute: 'And it is a rule that members must bathe on New Year's Day. And all members wear the club insignia, a winkle. It is a most heart-warming sight to see them dash into the sea, with the men wearing their winkles round their necks.'

As to running, Brendan Foster began a tremendous revival of the sport which created Gateshead Stadium on the way. Such men as Foster, McLeod, Cram, Spedding et al are the tip of the iceberg. At the height of his powers Foster declared, 'I am not even the best runner in Gateshead.' Whilst not wanting to call him a liar, I would have been surprised if anybody had emerged to prove his point. Unless it was the snoozer in front of the telly who suddenly realized it was five minutes to closing time and a mile and a half to go. (Old joke: 'What's Russian for a pint?' 'Five to ten.')

It is the run-of-the-mill runners who keep the sport going. The lads turn up each week just for sport, with no hope of winning anything.

But nowhere does the Geordie show his sense of humour more than in the tolerance he shows to his respective football club. Only a person with a sense of humour could accept the fare offered. Or a stoic.

Take the managers, please. Rowan Atkinson has

them off to a fine art. Northumbrian born, his Geordie football manager is so true as to be painful to a local supporter.

Speaking to an imaginary team he says, 'Thirty-two nowt, thirty-two nowt. But don't worry lads, there's still hope, it's only half-time.' And when he takes a football from the bag and asks the players what it is, there is an obvious sense of relief when a player can tell him.

Football managers are a separate breed of animal. Perhaps it is the north-east that affects them.

Take Lawrie McMenemy, successful ex-manager of Southampton, sparkling TV personality, jet setter – even spoken of in the same category as Brian Clough! And then he was cajoled into managing Sunderland F.C.

SUPPORTER: 'He said he would get them out of the second division in two seasons. He kept his word. He didn't specify which direction, mind you.'

The resilience of football managers is as amazing as the public's memory is short. McMenemy is back on the box as a guru. I suppose if you have been a football manager you have nerve for anything, if the job has not killed you. And I must say he looks all right. As well as McMenemy could, anyway. Mind you, I would not recommend that he return to Sunderland too soon, if ever.

Some years ago, Newcastle United had a football manager who was, to speak euphemistically, no Brian Clough. So what's new?

During the rain (and the word is used advisedly) of Bill McGarry on the Magpies, I had the pleasure of being after-dinner speaker for a conveyance of building societies. So I updated a twenty-(at least)-year-old gag.

Bill McGarry was walking past the Alliance Building Society offices when he slipped on a banana skin – an inbuilt habit. He banged his head, broke two paving stones and was knocked unconscious. The kindly staff, not realizing what, I beg your pardon, who, it was, carried him inside. On discovering his identity, they gave him immediate first aid, thus delaying his recovery by several hours. When he came round, he said faintly, 'Where am I?'

'You're in the Alliance,' he was told.

'Whatever happened to the third and fourth divisions?' he asked.

Although they use their native dialects, all football managers receive their public relations diplomas from the same source. 'I think it was a diabolical decision, and if the manager of the other team, who I shall not name like some I could mention but won't, is prepared to repeat that to my face instead of behind my back I'll make him smile on the other side of the coin, because all's fair in love and that, but in this case it definitely is not. And if he turns round and that and that's all I've got to say and he's got another think coming and that's final and that . . .' Except Brian Clough. And that's final on managers and that.

Nobody ever took Len Shackleton's place in my admiration as a footballer (George Best was the nearest) and nobody ever topped him in his summing up of directors. In his book on football, *Clown Prince of Soccer*, he had a page with the inscription, 'What the average football director knows about football' On turning the page, there it was – blank! Nuff said. I do not think it has changed. Not for the better, not in the north-east.

The most the teams can hope for is a position in the

middle of the first division. The fans, very knowledge-able, will turn out to watch. They live in hope. It is said that it is better to travel hopefully than to arrive. Which means that they will always have hope. But what is wrong with that? It means that the directors are there in perpetuity.

Yes, there is always hope. Except at Hartlepool. All the standard jokes apply there.

FAN: (*On telephone*) 'What time is the kickoff?'
CLUB SECRETARY: 'What time can you get here?'

When a fan, another one – they have two – asked the way to the ground he was told to follow the crowd and finished up in Woolworths.

The rivalry between Newcastle United and Sunderland must be on a par with the religious fervour of the two big Glasgow clubs. Without the religion to give it a legitimate basis for hatred. There are even people who have season tickets for both clubs. Apart from being wealthy, they must also be schizophrenics. Nothing else could explain it to a normal fan. It stands to reason. You can only be in love with one club at a time. It is still possible to start a bar-room brawl over the defection of Shackleton to Sunderland all those years ago. At least Hughie Gallagher and Supermac had the decency to defect down south. And wor Jacky went to Ireland, and Newcastle had had the very best years.

As big a cheer goes up for the announcement of a Sunderland defeat as for a home win at St James's Park. And vice versa at Roker.

A friend of mine explained it. 'You see,' he said, 'Sunderland is an upstart toon – nee background, Gateshead withoot the culture. They imitate wor bridge, wor football strip, wor football song. Nee originality.'

I tried to point out that it could be an inferiority complex.

'A what?'

'A chip on their shoulders.'

'Wey no man, that's their heads.'

What can you say? – as biased as a normal football fan.

Middlesbrough is tolerated by both clubs, presumably because it is no threat, and has yet to do anything of note. Far better to be despised, hated even, than tolerated – the badge of mediocrity.

Definition of a Sunderland fan: 'He reads the paper from the front.'

When Sunderland won the cup in 1973 (the first time this had been achieved from the second division), they beat the premier team of the time, Leeds United. The local television station showed the streets of Sunderland gradually becoming repopulated after the game. An amazing sight.

The following year Newcastle United reached the final to be humiliated by the emerging Liverpool. When the team returned to Newcastle it was cheered all the way from the Central Station to St James's Park. I think they did a lap of honour around Grey's Monument. In South America they would have been lynched. Justifiably.

During the cup final, Malcolm MacDonald appealed to the referee. 'Can we have another football?' he asked.

'What's wrong with the one you've got?' asked the ref.

'Liverpool's playing with it,' said Supermac.

Since then, the only moment of note was a quickie. Newcastle were playing Crystal Palace at home and were all over them. It was a novelty game. There was an announcement from the loudspeaker, 'Crystal Palace are to substitute Posse for Whittle.'

A voice from the crowd exclaimed, 'Posse – they need the bloody cavalry.'

I should mention Keegan, the miracle man who hauled Newcastle back into the first division. There was talk of adding another gospel to the *New Testament*.

When Keegan arrived, rumour had it that he only came up for the Great North Run. He was spotted, kidnapped, and was allowed his freedom as soon as Newcastle United were promoted.

Bob Bolam writes and performs 'in the dialect' of Northumberland. Blame him, not me, for a stuttering story. It is translated into English (sort of):

Hard L-L-Luck
A fella from wor colliery says,
B-B-Bye, I've had bad luck,
I ch-ch-chose a team there,
And I've really come unstuck.

The p-p-pools, I've been let down.
It was all reet, bar one team.
'Who was it?' ses his marrah
As they dandered to the seam.

'It was B-B-B.' 'Oh Bradford?'
'No, why no, they weren't my pick.'
'Why man B-B-B.' 'Oh, Barnsley?'
'Why not likely. Are you thick?'

'Bl-Bl-Bl.' 'Oh, Blackpool?
Blackburn Rovers? I give in.'
'Why man, Arsenal, BLOODY Arsenal,
Man, the beggars couldn't win.'

13 Strong Women: A Feature out of a Necessity

Frank E. Franks, Geordie comedian, said in 1940, 'Lord Haw Haw says that Hitler is going to come over here and fettle the local women. What a hope! The Geordie fellas have been trying to do that for years.' Which is true on both counts. After centuries of all forms of hardship, a world war can come as a relief and a release to the local women. It takes a remarkable female to put up with the lads round here. That's why they're put here, otherwise the beer-swilling, tab-smoking, darts-playing, leek-growing, pigeon-racing fraternity would be hard put to find somewhere to go at bedtime.

There are male chauvinist pigs, and there are Geordie male chauvinist pigs and the greater of these is the latter. Compared to him the others are just breast-feeding be-ginners, floundering on the foothills of male domination.

Under it all these great big tough he-men are not just little boys, but frightened little boys and the women know this and feed badly battered male egos with a show of affection by not showing any.

Val McLane and Anne Orwin were two of the originators of a remarkable community theatre group, *Live Theatre*. This is one of their duologues depicting a typical scene between two Geordie women:

STRONGWOMEN IN CABARET

Old Biddies Sketch

SADIE: There you are Alice, four books and a flyer. Hope it's our lucky night tonight.

ALICE: It's about time. I haven't had any luck since they called George up in 1939.

SADIE: Eeh what an awful thing to say. You'd miss him if he wasn't here.

ALICE: You are joking, of course.

SADIE: You would. You'd miss his company.

ALICE: Company? I'd get more company living with Houdini and he keeps disappearing. I don't know. Since he's retired I've had to work twice as hard. He keeps going on about having done his share. All those years up that crane in Vickers. Yer bugger he's on my back, breakfast, dinner and tea. He sits in that chair looking like Methuselah. He doesn't move unless it's to eat. He's murder, man.

SADIE: Well what about Albert? He's never in the house. He's always up the cree with his pigeons. I wish the bugger would move in with them.

ALICE: Here. Did you know Nancy Wilson's husband had died?

SADIE: No?

ALICE: Yes!

SADIE: Was it anything serious?

ALICE: No!

SADIE: Here. Are you coming to the Catholic bingo on Tuesday?

ALICE: If God spares iz.

SADIE: Oh divvent be so morbid, man. You're a long time gone.

ALICE: Aye and I'll not be in a hurry to come back either.

SADIE: Do you think you can?

ALICE: What?

SADIE: Come back?

ALICE: Why anything's possible nowadays. Who would have thought forty years ago there'd be men on the moon?

SADIE: I wish some of the buggers would stay there an' all. Here! If you could come back again what would you come back as?

ALICE: Oh a man! Definitely!

SADIE: Why? What would you do if you were a man?

ALICE: I wouldn't have to do anything would I? I'd have a wife.

SADIE: You wouldn't be able to have bairns.

ALICE: I've thought of that.

SADIE: Oh I don't think I'd like to be a man. You'd have to pretend you knew what you were talking about all the time.

ALICE: At least you could lose your temper without people accusing you of being hysterical.

SADIE: Aye that's true enough. Mind, I wouldn't like to have to shave every day.

ALICE: Why young lasses do that nowadays, lass – on their legs.

SADIE: Daft buggers! Here, I bet I know one who does – your Beattie.

ALICE: Oh aye. Bathtime Beattie. That lass is never done washing herself. She gets up in the morning and she's in the bath. She comes home for her dinner and she's in the bath. She comes home for her tea and she's in the bath. Before she goes out at night, she's in the bath. Wor Andrew came in the other night. He says, 'Where's wor Beattie?' and the budgie shouts: 'She's in the bath.' Here, did you tell your Albert that you won last week?

SADIE: Did I hell! All those years he was working I never even saw his pay packet. This is just between the two of us.

ALICE: Oh here comes Handsome Harry.

SADIE: Rattle them balls Harry. I could do with a win.

ALICE: Couldn't we all!

We have many well-kept secrets – the beauty of the region for one, assisted by Northern Arts grants to 'foreign' photographers. Leonard Barras is another. His profile is as low as a Tynemouth tide. He is the example of a regional writer sought out by the self-imported, self-important researchers who have spent all of two after-noons 'doing' the area. I hope one of them finds him. It will serve it right.

Leonard is a one-off, whose writings are peculiarly suited to performance, as BBC listeners to his short stories will testify. I used to believe I was the best

Strong women: Anne Orwin and Val McLane.

delineator of his work until I heard him reading these, which by no means diminishes my self-esteem. His style is deceptively deceptive, as was proved by a recent production of his play *Tight at the Back*, about football – what else? It was produced by the now defunct Newcastle Playhouse as a farce. The play is many things, but it is not a farce, and must be approached with great respect, greater caution and an internal application of broon (see glossary, if I remember to include it, broon being what it is).

Leonard is an anarchist, as anyone with half a mind can discern, which possibly excludes most theatre directors.

Herbert Mangle, the Wallsend poet, is a recurring inhabitant in Leonard's fertilely imagined, picturesquely decaying, coracle-building village on the banks of the picturesquely decaying Tyne with its picturesquely decaying MP (in what the locals refer to as 'a canny sittin' doon'). And a strong woman, if ever there was one (and there has been more than one) is Wallsend's Thelma Dutt. Perhaps a psychiatrist could explain Thelma's connection with Leonard and with Herbert.

With seatbelts firmly fastened, tongues firmly in cheeks, and cheeks firmly in seats (I may have met Thelma Dutt in another life), here's 'Public Exposures' from *Up the Tyne in a Flummox* by Leonard Barras:

> Herbert Mangle, the neo-Wordsworthian poet, used to claim that Councillor Mrs Thelma Dutt vied with the pit heap as Wallsend's noblest landmark. He was violently in love with her for three weeks, and one night was reading to her his 'Lines Written to a Vast Widow', when she perched on his knee and displaced a cartilage, rendering him unfit to keep goal for Wallsend Amnesia football team.
>
> My uncle Hal, Marxist team manager, upbraided this familiar Mangle surrender to the flesh and called on the Sunday School superintendent instead for the 'derby' match against Percy Main Static. The superintendent pointed out that he had a sprained thumb, sustained in striking the lectern during a sermon en-

titled 'Guard Thine Honour'. Nevertheless, he acknowledged that he smelt the battle far off and was willing to say among the trumpets, ha ha.

'That's all right then,' said Uncle Hal.

He would have preferred to hand the goalkeeper's jersey to Seppy Elphinstook, the celibate barber, who, because of his knock knees, seldom let a ball between his legs, but Elphinstook had lapsed into one of his misogynist spells, sitting in front of his fire, with his big toe sticking out of his sock, hating women.

'Mind you', Uncle Hall told my old Aunt Emma, 'the serious horrors are those which seem respectable to respectable men.'

'Eat your apple dumpling,' said my old Aunt Emma . . . When Seppy Elphinstook had been an eager young man in Hebburn, his father had planned for him a vaulting career as a tram inspector, but he hankered after the glamour of hairdressing and ran away to Wallsend, swearing that his immortal soul was not to be compromised.

Now, with the onset of middle age, he was sunk in disillusionment. Hairdressing had turned out to be less than fulfilling, and while the shop was full of shaggy customers, he would languish in his kitchen, dashing off wild water paintings of nude historical characters, in the time he could spare from hating women.

To Herbert Mangle, hating women was an alien philosophy. As it happened, even as he suffered his dislocated cartilage, he was about to break with Mrs Dutt anyway because he had just got engaged to the two ginger barmaids at the Dun Cow. When the rupture came, however, Mrs Dutt blamed it on Uncle Hal, her ancient adversary, and next day she cut him dead when she came on him standing on his hands down by the Gut.

There had been animosity between them since the council elections, when Uncle Hal had opposed her, standing as a Theoretical Nudist, his contention being that there was a pressing need for nakedness in politics. 'No politician', he told my Aunt Emma, 'could indulge in pompous dissimulation while the absurdities of his physique were plain to see.'

'The blood'll rush to your head,' said my old Aunt Emma. Thelma Dutt was a highly moral woman, president of the League of Decent Ladies, and she frequently censured the public exposure of footballers' knees. After a bitter election campaign, she had been returned with a majority of 897; Uncle Hall's eleven votes were cast by Wallsend Amnesia first team plus one reserve, Herbert Mangle spoiling his paper by writing on the back a sonnet to the Returning Officer's wife's buttocks.

Uncle Hal, while regretting his increasing shagginess, felt a distinct sympathy for Seppy Elphinstook, not least because he was himself a theoretical bachelor with theoretical nudist undertones. Shaw, he told my old Aunt Emma, had pointed out that marriage was a monstrous impediment, although we should all remember that when the Life Force beckoned, we had to follow.

'Have you seen my pudding cloth?' asked my old Aunt Emma. Just at that time, the Life Force had lured Uncle Hal into the Nonconformists' Philosophy and Ping Pong Group and he inaugurated his year of chairmanship by promoting an Art Exhibition, in the time he could spare from standing on his hands.

The reason why he performed daily handstands in

his football pants, bringing the blood to his head, was partly that he was in training for the 'derby' match and partly that the upside-down view across to the pit heap called out his austere love of primitive. It was this same craving for the natural life that had prompted him to take the job of temporary Turkish Baths attendant, pending the advent of Marxist society.

Seppy Elphinstook's submission to the Art Exhibition was a wild water painting depicting Sir Walter Raleigh introducing potatoes to England in the nude. Uncle Hal applauded this. Could Asquith, he asked Mrs Dutt, have denied the vote to women if he had stood naked at the Despatch Box?

Mrs Dutt said he was incorrigible, but she might at least redeem a misguided celibate, and she sped to the barber's shop, where she found Seppy Elphinstook sobbing softly over a nude of Nelson falling at Trafalgar. It was in that moment that the Life Force beckoned to a vast widow.

Meanwhile, Herbert Mangle's engagement to the two barmaids was broken off when he absent-mindedly read to them his lines dedicated to Mrs Dutt.

'If Helen's face could launch a thousand Ships, Ten thousand might be sunk by Thelma's hips.'

My old Aunt Emma never found her pudding cloth, and yet she steamed an apple dumpling on the eve of the football match, which may have been why Uncle Hal's shrunken football pants on that sorry occasion revealed some of the absurdities of his physique. The Sunday School superintendent was ordered off after calling the referee a latter-day Nebuchadnezzar, and Wallsend Amnesia lost 23-0.

The following Monday, Uncle Hal, demoralized by this and by Herbert Mangle's elopement with the nurse

The first time in Wallsend's history that a theoretical nudist had to guard his honour from a Decent Lady.

who had set his cartilage, entered the Turkish Baths and wandered in error into the ladies' department. The only occupant was Mrs Dutt and in the horrified three-and-a-half minutes before he fled, he verified the accuracy of Herbert Mangle's lines.

Next morning, he was hand-standing by the Gut in shrunken pants when Mrs Dutt came along. He gazed fixedly at the upside-down pit heap and waited to be cut down. As it transpired, however, it was the first time in Wallsend's history that a theoretical nudist had to guard his honour from a Decent Lady.

Not that the Life Force was to be denied. Mrs Dutt sped again to the barber's shop, and so it came that Seppy Elphinstook, joining the ranks of respectable men, painted a ruff around Raleigh's neck and succumbed, with mended sock, to matrimony. All it cost him was his immortal soul.

14 *Me and Wor Lad:*
Both Ends Meat

Can you remember the exact moment you were grown up? I can. It was the day me mother let me and wor lad do the Saturday night shopping. She hadn't been ower grand, 'cos she usually took wi with her to the market, or else Scotswood Road. But me, I preferred the market. I *could* say it was because of me latent appreciation of Dobson's architectural gem, the Grainger Market. I could, but it's only since I've seen some of the modern monstrosities, and not only in the north-east either, that I appreciate places like the market and Grey Street. No, it was the smell. And whenever I feel a bit off I still have a wander and a sniff.

Me mother called it the butcher market, and with good reason. They were there on every corner of every avenue.

Anyways, on this particular occasion we set off with our instructions wrapped 'round the money. When I think back, I shouldn't have felt all that grown-up, 'cos wor lad was there, and even in those days wor lad knew how many beans made five – aye, and big ones and all.

Apart from that, we'd been with me mother far ower many times not to know the drill. We were nothing if not observant – soaked up information like a pair of five shilling shoes on a clarty night.

Saturday night shopping was a question of timing. You see, on a Saturday the butcher market had to get rid of its meat – no fridges, and nobody bought meat on a Monday. That was the height of high living. So if you got your timing right you could get some real bargains. But mind, there was more than the cannies knew this, and the economic laws of supply and demand have been in operation longer than the London School of Economics dares admit. You know who I'm getting at – the professionals with strings of letters after their Hungarian-type names, who couldn't make a commercial decision to save their secure sinecures, let alone buy meat in the butcher market of a Saturday night. But I'm digressing. The point I'm making is: not too early and not too late – the lull before the closing down storm – and wor lad had it off to a tee.

Well, we walked down town, naturally – it was downhill and we were young and fit, and arrived at the market early. Like gladiators (tichy ones with squeaky shoes and invisible swords), we scented the arena – blood and sawdust, the authentic smell of the butcher market; a Roman holiday in a Geordie bullring with most of the gory exhibits laid out on display. I was a sensitive bairn, but the blood and carcases didn't offend me in any way and the pictorial similes only come as an afterthought from the warm reflections of nostalgia in a comfortable middle age.

At the time it was heaven, all the stores laid out with groceries, meat and poultry and there were even toy stalls. I loved those, full of little knick-knacks that came to pieces in five minutes; lead soldiers, and books.

Books! There was a bookstall there that drew me as a child, and still does, practically unchanged. Boxes with books in marked 'All in here one penny'. Every book ever written seemed to be there.

But wor lad liked the arcade with a balcony at one end. He was quite musical and was fond of a shop there with George Formby ukulele–banjos in it – he bought one some years later, and became a good little plonker. I've still got it and I can't play a note. At the other end of the arcade was the balcony. Below this, two cafes: 'Nice hot dinner for sixpence,' the canny soul outside used to shout. It was always my ambition to try one. An ambition since achieved, though for more than sixpence.

But how can you describe your particular paradise? It would save me a lot of trouble and purple patches of prose if you took a look at Grainger Market yourself. It's changed very little in appearance – probably as much a reflection of Geordieland as you're likely to get in these plastic-processed-cheese days. Mind, talking of cheese, there is still a real cheese stall in the arcade end where the bloke takes pride in his wares and enjoys his job. You can tell.

It was now zero hour, the time to watch prices closely. We had to get a nice bit of beef for Sunday dinner, some beef sausage, as much fat as we could get for nowt – for dripping, some 'ducks', black pudding and bacon for Sunday breakfast. Ducks? You've never heard of ducks?

You should think black burning shame, and find out before your ignorance overcomes you.

We did well, got everything at the right price, and at the same butcher's stall – a canny man who gave wi more than we had money for. I mind even wor lad was a bit taken aback.

'Gan on, me bonny bairns, let your mother see what clever lads ye are – she couldn't have done any better hersel'.' And mind, she couldn't.

We walked out into Nelson Street, past the Gaiety Cinema with a history of music hall dating back to mid-Victorian times, along to the top end of Grainger Street and round by Grey's Monument into Blackett Street just in time to catch a tram outside the YMCA.

'Howay, noo lads, up ye come.' A helping hand from the conductor and we were off. We paid wor ha'pennies straight away and went upstairs to the clanking of the bell. We'd just sat down when wor lad said, 'Seppy, where's the beef sausage?'

We searched, then I remembered, 'Wor Ernie, I left it in the butcher's.' Downstairs we scarpered.

'Mister? Can we get off and have wor ha'pennies back? We've left the sausage.' By now we were passing St Andrew's Cemetery in Gallowgate.

'I'm sorry, sonner, but I've given you your tickets.'

A penny was a lot to anybody in those days and the conductor couldn't afford to refund two daft little lads . . .

'Wey, Seppy, that's that.'

'I'm sorry, Ernie, we'll just have to get off.'

'What? And waste the tram fare? Seppy, we're going to get wor money's worth – we've paid now.'

And we did. All the way home to Stanhope Street in the tram. Then we walked all the way back to the market.

Me and wor lad.

The butcher was already locked up. His face lit up when he saw the pair of us trailing into the now empty market.

'I thowt ye'd be back. Here's your sausage.'

'Thank ye mister, it was his fault.'

I was very ashamed; after all, I was every bit of five.

So we walked all the way home again. Me, I was very tired, but just as relieved. I loved me Sunday sausage. It was done with the roast, hard, crisp and crunchy.

Me mother was getting worried by this time, so we told her what had happened.

'Aye,' she said, 'You'd paid. It was *your* ride.'

So that was all right, me mother didn't think Ernie's decision was illogical.

Come to think of it, neither do I. As she said, we *had* paid, hadn't we?

15 The Heritage Industry: Oh Con All Ye Faceless

In the 1960s Geordie folk singer Bob Davenport used to bring dude mines into his act, comparing them with dude ranches in American cowboy country. Now we have one for real at Beamish Museum. Soon there will be more dude mines than there are real ones at the present rate of so-called 'progress'.

It is now big business in the north-east, heritage. It's perhaps not so rewarding to the inhabitants as industry, but it's cleaner. It does not actually produce material things, it may not even produce morale, but it is here to stay. Who wants to be a living waxwork, a walking example? Soon the whole area could be one big museum.

'I say, how quaint – a working-class person, except of course he doesn't work.'

There is a huge man-made forest, Keilder, with a huge man-made lake, Keilder, and a huge man-made midge population to go with it. The lake was created to provide power and water for non-existent industry. It can now be used for leisure. Except that the people with enforced leisure can't afford to use it. And the forest? Apart from changing the landscape from its original appearance, it must have its uses. The border rievers would find it hard work to get through for a start. But they've been outmoded. The raiding today is done by more insidious forces – those who come and tell us of a better life. The sad part is that some of them are sincere.

Years ago, when southern acquaintances asked me what it was like in the north-east, I would reply, 'There's an awfully cold wind from the slag heaps.' And now slag heaps are a protected species. And we have to attract visitors or perish. Or so we are told. By our betters.

And yet a friend of mine visited Durham city, a tourist trap if ever there was one. Some never get away. He went to the local tourist information centre. It was closed. Of course it was. It was a holiday. Such nerve!

The area is wick with heritage. There is an amazing amount of it still around, despite the enthusiastic developers who are probably eyeing Durham Cathedral.

I can hear them now: 'We shall, as a matter of course, retain the façade. But that green is an absolute waste. A splendid dome between the cathedral and the castle making the whole concept one vast leisure centre – the Sanctuary Leisure Palace. Work for local actors as nuns and monks – Equity, of course. We can't go around upsetting the natives.'

As for culture! Where do they all come from? There they all are, at the drop of a grant. With a canny sinecure at a local educational centre to go with it.

But when it comes to the heritage of the everyday Geordie, things are very different. Napoleon said we were a nation of shopkeepers.

Today he would say that the north-east was one big shop. A while ago Europe's largest shopping precinct was built in Newcastle, 'inside out', as one local worthy explained, looking at all the blank external walls. We have gone from cornershops to shopping cities in living memory.

The cornershops were mini-markets. If they didn't sell it, it wasn't made. They even acted as the local medicine man, cutting out the doctor, who was thought of as a middleman. Between you and the undertaker. There were rows of pills on cards, pale pills for pale people, liver pills, stomach pills, pills to counteract the effect of too many pills.

LITTLE GIRL: 'Please can you take back the toilet roll for a loaf of bread? The company hasn't come.'

And all the childhood dares: 'Have you got any Wild Woodbines? Well tame them,' or 'Have you got any sly cakes? Well keep your eye on them.' And the ha'penny-long stands, and you wondered why you weren't being served. Only once. The learning you didn't get in school.

In those days the biggest shop you came across was the Co-op. With the 'divvy' that paid the gas bill every quarter. And they delivered groceries, would you believe, every Wednesday and you didn't have to pay till the Friday. The height of risk living. Just like the middle class, except we paid promptly. And if you took the order in on a Monday, you could pick up the goods there and then 'below the line'. And still not pay till Friday! 13216.

What was your 'store number'? You picked up the week's flour and yeast and tried not to eat all the yeast on the way home. You gave the game away if you bowked.

And now the MetroCentre is Gateshead's answer to those slurs down the years, beginning with John Wesley's description: that 'dirty back lane leading to Newcastle.'

Already local comedians are doing whole acts about it the Metro.

It's the car-parks. The car-parks! You queue to get in, you queue to get out, and the bit in the middle costs a bomb. And the shops. Everyone is selling you things that you've got to have and you don't need. And it's one long permanent sale. And even the sales have sales. And people dressed up as sales attractions.

But when it comes to shopping or housing for everyday Geordie: 'We want a bath in the new council house an' all. We need summick to keep the coals in.' A bath was a supposed requisite when rehousing was taking place between the wars – new slums for old.

SOCIOLOGIST: 'It takes two generations to educate families to the uses of modern council homes.'

DISILLUSIONED 'And how many generations to
OCCUPANT: educate the planners?'

I asked Ray Stubbs about the new housing scene. He said, 'Remember this, Joe. All these architects and planners have one thing in common. None of them live there.' I suggested they had the highest of motives – good intentions.

'Tell me about the pathway to hell. Have you seen Killingworth lately?' And he rested his case. It was a case of broon and I helped him lighten it.

Killingworth New Town was built in the early 1970s. The inhabitants claimed it was modelled on Alcatraz. Inquisitive investigators have only the plans to go from. The town was destroyed in 1987. The architect lived locally. But not in Killingworth New Town.

Peterlee in County Durham, was built with the best of intentions. As was Washington New Town. It has a fine arts centre which periodically disappears. I can only find it when I am performing there. Out of sheer desperation. I start off the day before. Eric Boswell wrote a song about it, which local school children sing. Geordie Washington came to find his ancestral home. Here is a snatch:

> 'I got lost off,' he says to me, 'In districts six and
> seven.'
> 'There's ower many signs aboot, it's nowt like this in
> heaven.'
> Aa says, 'Noo, I was born here, and I knaa the district
> well,'
> Just come along wi' me bonny lad.' Then I got lost
> mesel!

The old housing was dreadful. But you *could* find your way. And it wasn't the pathway to hell.

16 Pubs:
From Bare Necessity
to Plastic Palace

'I'm now ganna sing a song the length of Scotswood Road, sixty-four bars.' (Horace Nelson's comment made in the 1930s.) Now there are two. Lord Armstrong's 'traditional' armaments works on the banks of the Tyne are no longer there. Nor the workers. You had to stand back at the mid-day break – in they would pour to put back some of the moisture sweated out on the morning shift. Pint after pint was lined up on the counter, waiting – but not for long.

'By lad, the first one never touches the sides. It might as well be water.'

'Mebbees it is, I'd put nowt past these lads. Why don't we make the first one water? We could save on it.'

'If you're ganna talk like that I'm off. You'll be joining the Sally Army next.

I'm thirsty, not dirty.' Pubs were there to drink in, not enjoy. A very bare necessity.

Pub life is not what it was. Would you believe, in the Wooden Doll, North Shields on Sunday evenings, they have introduced a string quartet? To the incredulity of two ex-regulars:

'A what?'
'A string quartet. Ye knaa, they play music.'
'Wey man, wor club's got that. Last week – Ray Stubbs and his All Stars.'
'Nah, man, this is real music.'
'Divvin't let Ray hear you say that. Ye knaa what he thinks of owt but jazz.'
'I'd like to hear what he thinks of this lot. They use music, ye knaa.'
'How d'ya mean, like?'
'Ye knaa – dots.'
'Real dots?'
'Nee words, just dots.'
'Nee words? How do they knaa what they're playing?'
'They must have rehearsed.'
'Whatever next!'
'Aye, and nee amplification.'
'That explains it! Neebody hears them, then.'
'They dee, ye knaa. Neebody taaks, they arl sit and listen.'
'Nevvor in the world. Sit and listen? It cannot last.'
'Why for not?'
'It'll gan bust. Neebody'll buy any beer.'

In High Bridge, Newcastle there is a pub called the Duke of Wellington with some interesting historical information on its outside wall which I intend to stop and read

'I'll bet he drinks Carling Black Label!'

someday. So far I have always been in too much of a hurry to join the self-appointed Geordie Club inside. Journalists meet there. Although I served my heckle-stopping apprenticeship in the working mens' clubs, I do not attempt more than, 'What'll you have?' by way of witty repartee. And even that can bring forth startling requests.

It was here that I learnt that one does not buy beer. One hires it by the hour, which gets shorter and shorter as closing time threatens and room for fresh deliveries is required. As one local said, 'We're ower near Scotland for fairness.'

The Last Word

There he was, waiting his turn by the well the day they turned off the tap water, when a pal drove by with a horse and trap. Would Pincher like to come and watch a famous football 'derby'?

In a trice the buckets were hid and they were off at a spanking pace to Willington, where a good time was had by all, including the horse which rested till Monday morning.

But wasn't all hell let loose when the missus, answering the door, discovering the missing knight-errant, his knees pathetically sagging with the weight of the two buckets of water? You can bet your boots it was.

'Well, you see hinny, pet, it was rather a long queue,' murmured an apologetic Pincher.

* * *

About three centuries or so ago a bunch of lads of all ages from nineteen to sixty-one went down Dean and Chapter Colliery to do the impossible – shift a conveyor from one district to another and build it up in thirty-six hours flat.

The roof was low and spiky and by the time the conveyor had been stripped down in the old district the gang gratefully sank back for a bite of bait, relaxed and slipped into blessed oblivion.

Then clanged the voice of the gaffer 'Howay, lads'. Nobody stirred. 'Time to get up,' railed the gaffer. 'It's half past twelve and Monday's started.' Then up piped Paddy McNulty: 'Half past twelve? Monday? Well, there's the back of the week broke.'

And amid cleansing laughter we got ourselves started again. The impossible was achieved and the conveyor ran on time.

See what I mean? When lads like these stick their toes in, nothing on earth can shift them. In defence, immoveable; in attack, irresistible; that's your Geordie once he gets started. So look out for him coming, particularly if he's laughing.

From 'The Laughter of the Geordie' by Sid Chaplin.

The end.